The Accidental Fundraiser

THE CHARDON PRESS SERIES

Fundamental social change happens when people come together to organize, advo-
cate, and create solutions to injustice. Chardon Press recognizes that communities
working for social justice need tools to create and sustain healthy organizations. In
an effort to support these organizations, Chardon Press produces materials on
fundraising, community organizing, and organizational development. These
resources are specifically designed to meet the needs of grassroots nonprofits—
organizations that face the unique challenge of promoting change with limited staff,
funding, and other resources. We at Chardon Press have adapted traditional techniques to the circumstances of grassroots nonprofits. Chardon Press and Jossey-Bass
hope these works help people committed to social justice to build mission-driven
organizations that are strong, financially secure, and effective.

Kim Klein, Series Editor

The Accidental Fundraiser

A STEP-BY-STEP GUIDE TO RAISING

MONEY FOR YOUR CAUSE

Stephanie Roth
Mimi Ho

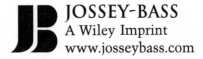

JOSSEY-BASS
A Wiley Imprint
www.josseybass.com

Published by Jossey-Bass
A Wiley Imprint
989 Market Street, San Francisco, CA 94103-1741   www.josseybass.com

The materials that appear in this book (except those for which reprint permission must be obtained from the primary sources) may be reproduced for educational/training activities. We do, however, require that the following statement appear on all reproductions:

The Accidental Fundraiser, by Stephanie Roth and Mimi Ho
Copyright © 2005 by Stephanie Roth and Mimi Ho

This free permission is limited to the reproduction of material for educational/training events. Systematic or large-scale reproduction or distribution (more than one hundred copies per year)—or inclusion of items in publications for sale—may be done only with prior written permission. Also, reproduction on computer disk or by any other electronic means requires prior written permission. Requests to the Publisher for permission should be addressed to the Permissions Department, John Wiley & Sons, Inc., 111 River Street, Hoboken, NJ 07030, 201-748-6011, fax 201-748-6008, or online at http://www.wiley.com/go/permissions.

Limit of Liability/Disclaimer of Warranty: While the publisher and author have used their best efforts in preparing this book, they make no representations or warranties with respect to the accuracy or completeness of the contents of this book and specifically disclaim any implied warranties of merchantability or fitness for a particular purpose. No warranty may be created or extended by sales representatives or written sales materials. The advice and strategies contained herein may not be suitable for your situation. You should consult with a professional where appropriate. Neither the publisher nor author shall be liable for any loss of profit or any other commercial damages, including but not limited to special, incidental, consequential, or other damages.

Readers should be aware that Internet Web sites offered as citations and/or sources for further information may have changed or disappeared between the time this was written and when it is read.

Jossey-Bass books and products are available through most bookstores. To contact Jossey-Bass directly call our Customer Care Department within the U.S. at 800-956-7739, outside the U.S. at 317-572-3986, or fax 317-572-4002.

Jossey-Bass also publishes its books in a variety of electronic formats. Some content that appears in print may not be available in electronic books.

Library of Congress Cataloging-in-Publication Data

Roth, Stephanie, date.
  The accidental fundraiser : a step-by-step guide to raising money for your cause / Stephanie Roth, Mimi Ho.
    p. cm.—(The Chardon Press series)
  Includes bibliographical references.
  ISBN-13 978-0-7879-7805-1 (alk. paper)
  ISBN-10 0-7879-7805-1 (alk. paper)
  1. Fund raising. I. Ho, Mimi, date. II. Title. III. Series.
  HG177.R68 2005
  658.15'224—dc22
                              2005017234

Printed in the United States of America
FIRST EDITION
PB Printing   10 9 8 7 6 5 4 3 2 1

CONTENTS

As we were writing this book, we found ourselves in many conversations about it with friends and family members who neither work for nonprofits nor are particularly involved in fundraising. When they heard the book was about how people who aren't fundraisers can raise money for a cause they believe in—like their kid's school or some other community effort—we started hearing story after story about something they or someone they knew had done to raise money for a cause.

Here are some stories we heard that convinced us there was a need for this book.

- Stephanie's nieces periodically ask her to buy wrapping paper or chocolate, or to sponsor them in a readathon to support their *public* school, that is, a school that is supposed to be supported by our tax dollars.

- An immigrant from El Salvador wanted to raise money quickly to send to a relief organization in his home town after a severe earthquake destroyed much of the community.

- A few friends in Minneapolis got together to help raise money for a candidate running for the local school board.

- A young Jewish woman from Boston returned from a trip to the Middle East with an interest in raising money to support a peace organization there made up of both Israelis and Palestinians.

- Colleagues who are community organizers in low-income communities in the United States need to raise money each year to send people to the World Social Forum, an annual conference that brings together low-income people working for social justice around the world.

Fundraising has become commonplace in the United States, in part because so many public institutions (schools, libraries, parks) that had been completely supported by taxes are facing budget cuts as government has abdicated responsibility for meeting even the most basic of community needs. The result is that more and more programs that were supported by our tax dollars are now seeking financial help from individuals, local businesses, and private foundations. That means more and more of you are being asked to help raise that money.

On a more positive note, people are also raising money because, as in the examples above, they are moved by a pressing community need, by a desire to make a difference in the world, or just to come together with their neighbors to improve the conditions in which they live. They decide they want to do something: organize a local theater group, clean up a toxic site in the neighborhood, lobby the city council for better lighting at night, get their community to provide better services to survivors of domestic violence, or provide more books and teaching materials for their local schools. In order to accomplish these projects—some of which are short-term, while others will take years to complete—they realize they need to bring people together to make it happen. They need people to participate by giving their time, and they need some of them to contribute some money as well.

This book was not written for professional fundraisers, though if you fall in that category you may find some good fundraising ideas here that you haven't tried before, and you are likely to find things here that are helpful to your volunteer team. It was not written for people working in nonprofit organizations who need to create the systems, infrastructure, and technology required to carry out sophisticated fundraising programs on an ongoing basis. This book is written for anyone—like *you*—who finds themselves unexpectedly needing to raise some money to carry out a particular project, activity, or event. It might be a time-specific need, such as attending a conference, or helping support emergency relief, or building a community center. Or it might be something that starts out as a one-time effort and then grows into an ongoing activity because you find yourself thrilled with what you were able to accomplish.

You might be a political activist or a member of a community organization, and while you never thought that raising money was something you'd ever agree to do, you finally agree at least to help out.

Or maybe you're a board member of a nonprofit organization and have learned that board members are expected to help raise money. If you don't really know where to start, this book should help steer you in the right direction.

The fundraising strategies described here are ones that a small group of people can organize and carry out, whether to fulfill their responsibility as board members or just because they want to participate in your organization in a meaningful way.

Oakland, California
June 2005

Stephanie Roth
Mimi Ho

ACKNOWLEDGMENTS

This book is the result of much collaboration, which is fitting for a work that stresses the importance of people coming together to make a difference with their time and their money. Many of the fundraising strategies we describe here were originally written about by others. We adapted them to provide a greater level of detail and "how-to" for readers who are primarily volunteers carrying out these fundraising strategies in their free time. We thank Californians for Justice, Rebecca Francis, Lucy Grugett, Kim Klein, Dennis Quirin, Mark Toney, and Blake Ulveling, for the use of their materials. In addition, we are grateful to the many people who sent stories about their fundraising successes in response to a request in the *Grassroots Fundraising Journal*'s e-newsletter and the many people in our trainings who have told us wonderful stories of their efforts. Their names would fill another book.

The original idea for this book came from Johanna Vondeling, our former editor at Jossey-Bass. Johanna convinced us that this book needed to be written and that, while there are many books on fundraising, few are written explicitly for volunteers, community members, and activists. Johanna's vision and support for this project made all the difference; we especially thank her for her willingness to give extremely useful feedback on the first draft, even after leaving Jossey-Bass. In addition, we are inspired by Johanna's refusal to compromise her principles and her willingness to take a stand.

Four other readers—Lisa Moore and three anonymous ones—reviewed an early draft of the book and gave valuable feedback that we greatly appreciated.

Nancy Adess, our copyeditor, works magic with all the words she touches, and we thank her for making sense of the many and varied elements in the book. We also thank our colleagues at Jossey-Bass—Dorothy Hearst, Allison Brunner, and Xenia Lisanevich—for bringing the book to life and making sure people hear about it.

Our thanks also go to the many organizations and people we've worked with over the years who have put these ideas and more to work raising money for great causes. They were an inspiration and a reminder that fundraising really can be done in all kinds of communities by all kinds of people. We especially acknowledge the commitment to raising money from a broad base of individual donors by organizations we've been very close to over the years: the Astraea Lesbian Foundation for Justice, Californians for Justice, the Center for Anti-Violence Education, and Jewish Voice for Peace.

From Stephanie

My thanks to the staff of the *Grassroots Fundraising Journal*—Nan Jessup, Adena Chung, and Jennifer Emiko Boyden—for keeping things going when I was distracted by book-writing deadlines. They are all amazingly talented and dedicated members of the *Grassroots Fundraising* team.

I thank my family for all of the great fundraising stories they shared (some of which made it into the book) and for their enthusiasm for this project. My thanks to my nieces, Emma and Alex, and to my friend Netsy's children, Sari and Molly, who started raising money from me and Kim as soon as they could talk, and to my friend Ellen's daughter, Sophie, who is learning to get over her fear of asking at the ripe age of eight.

I also thank Judith Pollock, my neighbor, friend, and physical therapist, whose healing hands kept my repetitive-stress injury under control so I could finish writing.

I thank my coauthor, Mimi, for agreeing to take on what neither of us knew would be such a consuming project, and for being such a thoughtful, thorough, and wonderful partner in writing.

And finally, I thank my life partner, Kim Klein, for her constant encouragement and good humor, especially in those moments when my frustrations were running high and I was tempted to give up altogether. She read every chapter at various points in their development, gave invaluable feedback, and did more than her fair share of housework to give me time to write. Her significant contributions to the current body of knowledge in fundraising are well known, and many of them inform the perspective of this book. More important to me than all of that is her love and support of the past sixteen years.

From Mimi

I want to thank Californians for Justice (CFJ) for instilling a deep commitment to grassroots fundraising as a critical part of building a movement for social change that genuinely contends for power. When CFJ began to fight the attack on affirmative action during the "No on 209" campaign, we literally built the campaign dollar by dollar, house party by house party, with thousands of people we met on the streets. I thank Kim and Stephanie for being mentors, colleagues, and friends to me through the years. They have been donors, trainers, consultants, phonebankers, volunteers, and doorknockers for many of the organizations I have worked with.

Personally, I want to thank my friend Manami Kano for great conversation—from the politics of fundraising and how to build a relevant and sustainable movement to the ridiculous, late-night conversations that kept me sane as I wrote this book. My partner, Ernest, has been an incredible resource—professionally as a colleague and personally as someone who grounds and sustains me in all aspects of my life. And finally, I thank all the gutsy, principled, supportive organizations, mentors, friends, and family who I have been lucky enough to have in my life. Thank you for keeping me on this path.

—S. R. and M. H.

HOW TO GET THE MOST FROM THIS BOOK

If your fundraising goal is less than $2,000, you can probably use any one of the strategies described in the following chapters. If you need to raise a larger amount, you will most likely use a few different strategies over a period of several months or a year.

The fundraising strategies described in this book are organized into three categories of approaches:

Asking people directly for money (personally, through phonebanking, and going door-to-door)

Holding social gatherings (house parties, community dinners, bowlathons and similar events, and auctions)

Selling (ad books, car washes, raffles, and garage sales)

We assume that you will be carrying out these activities with an all-volunteer group and that you are probably a volunteer yourself. For that reason, we've provided as much detailed "how-to" information as possible, with worksheets and forms you can adapt for your particular situation and with an approach that keeps the process as simple and manageable as possible for people who are doing these activities in their spare time.

Each chapter in Part Two, Fundraising Strategies, begins with a discussion of the best uses of that strategy and things to consider in deciding whether it's a good strategy for your group to take on. Next, there is a summary list of steps in carrying out the strategy, followed by a detailed discussion of each of the steps. The steps for each strategy are quite similar and generally consist of the following:

1. Make a plan

2. Recruit volunteers

3. Prepare materials (and find a location)

4. Decide whom to solicit for support

5. Complete final preparations for the activity

6. Hold the activity

7. Evaluate the activity and thank people

Each of the strategy chapters then ends with a sample workplan that gives you a "snapshot" of these key tasks and a proposed timeline for implementation. The workplans give you a quick and easy way to see the order in which tasks should be completed and approximately how long each should take. Use these workplans as guides from which to develop your own plan and timeline.

For some strategies, you'll need to find out about any special legal requirements or restrictions that may apply. For example, door-to-door fundraising, also called canvassing, is restricted or must be licensed in some communities; with car washes, you can run into problems if you don't dispose of the wastewater properly. Such special considerations are discussed in the relevant chapter.

Each strategy in this book will work better under some circumstances than others. Some are better if you have lots of volunteers available to help out, even if what they're willing to do is limited (selling raffle tickets or donating items for a garage sale or an auction). Other strategies are better if you have lots of people you could ask to support your cause (phonebanks, personal asks). And still others are better if you have a group of people who like to socialize with each other (special events, house parties). Regardless of the people needed to make a strategy successful, we have included only fundraising strategies that a great many groups of all sizes have used successfully, with volunteers carrying them out.

Another element that varies depending on the strategy you use is how important it is that the people you're asking to support your cause care deeply about the issue. For drivers to get their cars washed, the cause you want them to support may not be as important as the fact that their car is dirty, your location is convenient, or the timing works for them. For someone to agree to make a contribution in response to your fundraising letter and phone call, it will be more important that they support the cause or that they are motivated by their relationship with *you* and therefore support your efforts to raise money. For someone to make a large contribution, they will need to have strong feelings for the cause.

Finally, you will be most successful at whatever activity you choose if you can get others to help carry it out. Therefore, you might choose a strategy that doesn't make the most sense to you based on your analysis of the factors to weigh in making that decision, but if it's the one your team of volunteers is most excited (or just willing) to do, then it may be the best choice.

CHOOSING THE RIGHT STRATEGY

In deciding which of the fundraising strategies described in this book is the right one for you, there are several things to consider aside from the interest of volunteers. They include how much lead time you have to organize the activity, how many people you can recruit to help out, how much money you need to raise, and how many people you can find to ask.

The accompanying Fundraising Strategies Grid gives you a brief overview of what to expect from each strategy to help you in choosing the one or ones you may want to carry out. Keep in mind that the ranges given for lead time, number of volunteers needed, and so on are estimates of what is reasonable to expect. Each of these strategies can be used to raise more money than we've indicated here, but they may also raise less. Make sure to read through the chapter that describes the strategy you're interested in taking on to get a better sense of what it takes to be successful at raising the money you need.

In addition to the specific fundraising strategies that make up the bulk of this book, Chapter Two is devoted to getting others to join your fundraising efforts (Building Your Fundraising Team), Chapter Three addresses the importance of showing appreciation to your supporters (The Importance of "Thank-You"), and Chapter Four covers things to consider if your one-time effort turns into a longer-term endeavor (Beyond One-Time Fundraising). The tips you'll gain from reading these chapters will guide you through the challenges that arise in any new undertaking and will even help make your fundraising efforts fun.

Fundraising Strategies Grid

Strategy	Lead time	Amount that can be raised (net)	Number of volunteers needed	Number of people to ask	Response rate[a]
Personal ask	2–6 weeks	$250–$5,000	1–5	10–100	40%–50%
Phonebank	6–8 weeks	$250–$2,000	5	200–400	5%–10%
Door-to-door	4–6 weeks	$250–$2,000	6–10	200–500 households	5%–10%
House party	4–6 weeks	$500–$1,500	1–2	50–100	30%
Community dinner	12 weeks	$1,000–$3,000	10–15	200	20%
Bowlathon	8–10 weeks	$1,000–$2,500	7–10	100–300	25%–50%
Auction	12 weeks	$250–$3,000	10–15	200	20%
Ad book	12 weeks	$500–$2,000	10	200	5%
Car wash	3–6 weeks	$400–$500	5–8	Busy street	N.A.
Raffle	10–12 weeks	$1,000	20	400	50%
Garage sale	6–8 weeks	$300–$1,500	3–10	Busy street	N.A.

[a]This is the percentage of all the people you ask who will respond with a contribution.

USING THE TOOLS IN THIS BOOK

In order for this book to be as useful as possible, we've created several tools that you can photocopy and use to plan and organize your fundraising activities. The following are included in each chapter with examples of how you might use them and worksheets, workplans, and scripts are also available as blank, ready-to-use forms in Resource G.

 Worksheets and Workplans: These are forms that help you (and your volunteers) plan your project, track your progress, and organize information about who is supporting your efforts.

 Scripts: These are samples of conversation you can use on the phone or in person in your fundraising efforts. The blank forms at the end of the book are for tailoring the scripts for your own organization.

 Handouts: These are ready-to-use documents that you can photocopy for your volunteers, give to potential donors, and so on. They include tips and sample lists.

The Accidental Fundraiser

PART ONE

Fundraising ABCs

Part One is useful to read before you choose a fundraising strategy to carry out. The information in these chapters provides a context for understanding how fundraising works, the elements of successful fundraising, and how to get the most out of whatever strategy you choose. These chapters present an important reminder that fundraising isn't just about money, but about building relationships, carrying out a vision, and strengthening community.

Chapter One discusses basic fundraising principles and tips to help you get over your fear of asking for money. In Chapter Two you'll learn how to recruit other people to help, because you'll always raise more money and have more fun if you make fundraising a group effort. You'll also get useful tips for how to work as a team and how to deal with the challenges that arise within any group of people. Chapter Three reminds you of a lesson you probably learned as a child—that thanking people is important. Not only is it the right thing to do, but it tells the people who contributed to your cause that their support made a difference and increases the likelihood that they'll be willing to give again in the future. You'll also find sample thank-you letters that you can adapt for your own situation. Chapter Four addresses the kinds of things you'll want to think about if you decide to do ongoing fundraising. These include how to keep track of your donors and volunteers and how to document what you learned from your fundraising efforts so that you can revise and refine your strategy when you go back to do it again.

We hope the chapters in this part will inspire and motivate you to set ambitious goals and to take the time to make a plan that is both realistic and achievable. You'll learn that you *can* raise money and that millions of people are engaged in doing just that every day.

You *Can* Ask for Money

You probably picked up this book because, like so many people in communities around the country, you have found yourself in the unexpected position of needing to raise money for something and you want to find the easiest, quickest way to do that. Like so many skills, raising money is one anyone can learn, and just jumping in and trying out some new things is probably the best way to learn. But unlike some other skills (such as learning to read, cook, ride a bicycle, or use a computer), very few people are excited to learn this one. This book will help you get a little more excited about learning how to raise money, and it will also make the process easy and straightforward.

Fundraising gets a bad rap in our society. Just ask any professional fundraiser what kind of response they get when people find out what they do for a living. Most will tell you they are regarded with suspicion. Though people are usually too polite to ask, "Why would you choose *that* line of work?" many regard raising money as slightly sleazy or at least distasteful. These reactions seem to be bound up with the idea that we shouldn't talk about money or mention the topic except under specifically prescribed situations.

On the other hand, start talking about community-based fundraising activities— from walkathons and car washes to pancake breakfasts—and almost anyone you talk to will have a story about something they or someone they know did to raise money. Unfortunately, this is partly because programs that used to be funded entirely by the government, and for which we pay taxes, are now facing such shortfalls in their budgets that they are forced to turn to the private sector for support. This includes public schools, public parks, and even public health departments. But there are also people who are inspired to make the world a better place and need money to fund a new idea or project toward that end. These are people who don't necessarily work in a nonprofit organization or consider themselves fundraisers, but they realize that fundraising will help them achieve their goals.

MORE THAN MONEY

When you engage in an activity to raise money for something you care about, you will find that the process of asking people for money involves educating them about an issue and raising their awareness about something they may not have known about. A corporation in your community is found to be dumping toxic waste into a local river and by raising money to organize people to stop them, your community organization also raises awareness about the problem. When you start communicating either one-on-one to your friends and neighbors, or through the media, or by holding a public fundraising event, you spread the word about your cause far beyond the relatively small group of people who devote much of their time to the work.

People Like to Give

What do we make of these seemingly contradictory messages and feelings about money and specifically about fundraising? The most important thing to keep in mind is that people actually like to give money to things they care deeply about. When we conduct workshops on how to raise money for community organizations around the country, we often ask the workshop participants how many feel good when they make a contribution to an organization or cause they care about. Almost everyone raises their hand. When we ask the same people how many feel good asking a friendly, supportive person to give money to their cause, very few people raise their hand. This tells us, not surprisingly, that people are more comfortable giving than asking.

So if you focus your attention more on the good feelings people get from giving and less on your own discomfort with asking, you'll find asking for money a lot easier. Remember that people are going to give money away, and if you don't ask them to support something you think they would care about, someone else will.

People Want to Make a Difference

Fundraising is about more than just getting the money you need to do the thing you want to do. Although that's what gets most of us started on the fundraising road, what really motivates people to give is the extent to which they feel moved or touched by an issue. The tragedy of the tsunami in South Asia at the end of 2004 resulted in an enormous outpouring of support from people all over the world. People gave because they wanted to participate in responding to an unprecedented global disaster with positive action. They wanted to make a difference, and giving money was the easiest and most important way they could do so.

You Know People Who Want to Give

Most of the strategies described in this book require you to tap into networks of potential donors that you and your team or group or organization already know. This may cause you to exclaim, "But I don't know anyone with money!" We can assure you that this isn't true. For one thing, studies have shown that seven out of ten Americans give away money. This includes people of all class and race backgrounds, all ages, sexes, and sexual orientations. That means at least some of the people you know (probably about 70 percent of them) already support causes they care about. Moreover, most of the people who give donate to several different organizations.

We recognize, however, that there are cultural differences in how people relate to each other and how groups function. It is not a requirement for successful fundraising that all requests for support be done in a certain way. Think about what kinds of approaches will work in your community—whether it's better to be more direct or less direct, more specific or more general, and so on. Most important to understand is that there are few absolutes in fundraising. Fundraising is like many other activities that we carry out in our lives without thinking about them— we know what will offend people and what will make them feel good, what will make them feel excluded or included in a group, and what will make them want to give money to an organization that is working for something they believe in. In all cultures, people get together to accomplish goals, make change, and raise money to do so.

GETTING OVER THE FEAR OF ASKING

Kim Klein, nationally acclaimed fundraising trainer and author, writes about the psychological barriers to asking for money. We have found the following insights she explores in *Fundraising in Times of Crisis* extremely useful in helping people overcome their reluctance to ask for money:

1. *If you want money, you have to ask for it.* While there are some people who will simply send an organization money or offer money without being asked, most people will not think to give you money unless

you make your needs known. This is not because they are cheap or self-centered; it is because most people have no idea how much it costs to run a nonprofit organization or how nonprofits get money. If you don't ask them, they will simply assume you are getting the money you need somewhere else.

2. *It has to be OK with you for people to say no.* Your job is to ask, to offer people the opportunity to give to your group. The person being asked also has a job; their job is to take you up on your offer or to turn you down. What they do will depend on their mood, their financial circumstance, their other commitments—many variables that you can't do anything about and that are not about you or your group. People who say no may say it directly: "No, I can't help you." They may say no by never responding to your letters or calls. They may say no by saying, "I'll think about it" and never get back to you. And they even may say no by saying yes and then never pay their pledge. Nonetheless, enough people will say yes to make it worth continuing to ask. But you must ask far more people than the number of gifts you need.

3. *What you believe in has to be bigger than what you are afraid of.* If you don't like asking for money, or you would rather not do it, or you wish someone else would do it for you, that is normal. That is how most people are. But I suggest you think about what is going to happen if you don't ask anyone for money. What will happen to your organization? Does it matter if your organization goes out of business? If it matters to you, then put that first, ahead of your anxiety about asking. There is an old fundraising saying, "If you are afraid to ask for money, kick yourself out of the way and let the cause talk."

4. *You will need to ask some people, but you don't need to ask everyone.* Many people never get out of the starting gate because they think they have to ask everyone they know. Don't ask people you have a difficult relationship with or who don't believe in your cause. Start with someone very easy: yourself. Make your own gift first. Make sure your gift is significant for you—that you feel it and it

feels good. Then go to friends and family members whom you like, who like you, and who agree with the cause you represent.

5. *Put yourself in the donor's shoes.* You may not like asking, but that doesn't mean the donor doesn't want to be asked. Most people like to be seen as helpful and generous. They like to be included. Sometimes organizations go out of business and people around the organization will say, "I never knew they were in trouble. Why didn't they ask for help?" There are far more hurt feelings from not being included and not being asked than there ever will be from being asked.

MAKING YOUR CASE FOR SUPPORT

Before you start asking people you know for money, as well as asking them to join you in asking others for money, you need to be able to make a case for why people should give to your cause. Often we get so involved in an issue or project, we forget that other people don't necessarily understand the importance, or urgency, or even the impact of the issue we're working on. We lapse into jargon or phrases that only those of us working closely on the project really understand.

So along with coming up with a solid plan, clearly defined tasks, and a group of people willing to carry them out, you also need a way to describe what you're raising money for that draws the attention and interest of the people you're trying to raise money from. Put yourself in their shoes as you imagine making a pitch to them. What would move you to respond favorably to a request? What would stand out in your mind about what that person said?

Most important in coming up with a message is that it's brief—you can say it in two or three sentences—and that rather than answering the question, "What does your group do?" it answers two other questions: "Why is this work important or necessary?" and "How can I help?" Here are a few examples:

For a community health fair: "We believe that people want to be healthy, but lack the information and choices for eating better and exercising more. The quality of our air, land, and water are also part of what makes a community healthy, and we need to learn how we can hold government and business accountable to our health. We're planning a community health fair to provide a range of information about personal and community resources for making our lives and the life of our community stronger and healthier. We hope you'll support this event with a contribution."

For a community arts project: "We believe that art is not just something you see in a museum; it is the expression of the creative impulse that exists in all of us. By providing opportunities for people to learn how to express their creativity in a nonjudgmental setting, we see them transform their lives in amazing and wonderful ways."

To enable a member of an environmental justice project to attend a national conference: "As the toxics dumped by local industry in our town's landfill are affecting the water quality in our predominantly African-American community, we are starting to fight back. Can you help us send some of our most active community members to a national conference that is working to build a grassroots response to industrial pollution?"

MAKING YOUR FUNDRAISING SUCCESSFUL

Each fundraising strategy in this book has its pros and cons, things that make it better for some communities or situations than others. As you skim through the chapters to decide which strategies you want to try, you'll see that paying attention to the following common features will help you be successful in raising money.

Find a group of people to participate in the fundraising activity. It can be a small group—even two or three people is preferable to your doing it all yourself. Working with a team will allow you to raise more money, expand the network of contacts who will ultimately lead you to more gifts, and be more fun.

Set a goal and create a plan. Different strategies require different amounts of lead time. Make sure you have enough time to carry out the tasks that will produce a successful outcome. A plan will give you the confidence that the goal you're trying to reach is actually realistic (even if also ambitious). Each strategy in this book includes a sample workplan and timeline at the end of the chapter describing it so you can see exactly what's involved and the kind of time you'll need.

Have one person (or at most two) to coordinate the work. You may have a team of the most responsible and reliable people helping out, but having one or two people who keep on top of the details, stay in touch with everyone on the team, and encourage them along will make all the difference.

Be sure to thank everyone involved. Remember to include your volunteers as well as the people who donate money. Thanking people isn't just the right and respectful thing to do, it will make it possible for you to go back to volunteers and donors and ask them to help again in the future.

Keep in mind that fundraising is really about relationships. Even if your plan is only to do this "one-time" activity and never agree to participate in another fundraising project ever again, how you relate to everyone you work with is important. Keeping relationships in mind means helping make the experience of volunteering, asking for money, and donating money to your cause a positive one so that people feel good about the experience and remain open to being involved in other causes in the future.

IN-KIND CONTRIBUTIONS

Often what you most need, either to make a fundraising activity net more money or in place of something that costs money, is something that a small business or larger corporation might be willing to donate. Some projects depend almost entirely on a combination of time from volunteers and items from businesses, unions, and nonprofits, with very little cash exchanged.

Many of the strategies described in this book count on at least some of the support to come from in-kind contributions. These include raffle prizes, auction items, office space (with lots of phones) to do a phonebank, a community center or parking lot to hold a garage sale or other event, printing and photocopying services, design services for your invitations and fliers, and food and drink for various events.

As you're putting together your budget, include in-kind contributions wherever you can. You also need to have a back-up plan for the possibility that you'll have to pay for something you'd hoped would be donated, but be sure to ask for donated goods and services first.

People usually find it easier to ask for an in-kind donation than to ask for money. Identify the volunteers who are more reluctant to ask for money and find out if they would be willing instead to solicit in-kind donations.

NOT BEING A NONPROFIT ORGANIZATION

You may be a volunteer or staff member of an established (large or small) organization that is incorporated as a nonprofit and has federal tax-exempt status with the tax designation 501(c)3. However, it is perfectly legal to raise money without being part of a nonprofit organization—if you understand a few basic things.

First, you need to decide how you are going to collect and manage the money that you raise. You have two choices, each of which have implications for whether your donor can get a tax deduction for their gift.

Find a nonprofit organization in your community that is willing to be your fiscal sponsor. That means they will receive the money, deposit it in their bank account, keep track of it, and then give you the money raised, minus a small fee (usually 6 percent to 10 percent of what you bring in) to handle their administrative costs. The advantage of this option is that the people making a contribution can get a tax-deduction for their gift, and they may feel more assured that their money is being well used. Of course, if someone is paying for a car wash or purchasing an item at a garage sale or auction, their payment is *not* a tax-deductible contribution because their payment is in exchange for goods or services received. If they're buying a ticket to your community dinner, you must deduct the fair-market value of that dinner from the ticket price when calculating how much of the donation is tax-deductible for the donor. So, for example, if the dinner you're serving would sell for $25 in your community, and the ticket price is $40, the portion of that ticket that is tax-deductible to your donor is $15, not the total cost of $40.

Open your own bank account. In this case *none* of the contributions people make to you will be tax-deductible. For many people this will not matter, but for larger gifts, donors may be unwilling to make a donation that is not tax-deductible. Moreover, if you go this route, your donors will need to trust that you are doing what you say you will with the money. Without the legal structure of a nonprofit organization, you do not have to meet the requirements of providing financial information to anyone who requests it or to report your financial activities to the government every year.

Note that if you're raising funds for a political campaign (either for a political candidate or a ballot initiative), keep in mind that donations to political electoral campaigns have stricter reporting laws, so check the laws of your state and region. The Federal Political Practices Commission requires that donors who give more than $250 over the course of an election cycle must inform the commission of their employer and occupation.

With this background in mind, you're ready to find the fundraising strategy that fits best with what you're trying to accomplish and who you can recruit to participate in the project. Go for it, and good luck!

Building Your Fundraising Team

All of the strategies described in this book will raise more money as you involve more people. This chapter describes the process of creating and building a successful fundraising team. By working with some basic principles of team building, you will be able to recruit people to your fundraising project, make the experience a positive one for everyone, and even leave people looking forward to their next opportunity to work together. While very few people would say they love to ask for money, it is possible to make fundraising fun, and paying attention to the needs of your fundraising team will make all the difference.

RECRUITING PEOPLE TO YOUR FUNDRAISING TEAM

People volunteer for different reasons:

- They believe strongly in something and want to help
- They want to be part of a group, especially one in which people they like and respect are involved
- They want to support the person who asks them to join
- They like to feel needed
- They want to contribute a skill they know would be helpful to the cause
- They don't really want to, but feel that they should

When inviting people to join, think about who they are and what motivates them. If you know that you're talking to someone who loves a party and the social aspect of any activity, tell them who else you're inviting to participate in this fundraising project and why this will be a great group to work with. If you're recruiting someone who likes to feel needed, make sure they know their participation would make a difference and how much it would mean to you to have them involved. With someone who believes strongly in the issue you're raising money for, talk about the importance of the cause. In any case, don't just send out an e-mail or place a notice in your newsletter and wait for people to volunteer. Actively reach out to people and make the recruitment process as personal as possible. Once you have a few volunteers, let others know who is on the team. People will be more likely to join if others they like and respect have already done so.

Find the right balance between deciding everything about the project ahead of time and bringing people together with the question, What should we do? If you've already decided what fundraising strategy you're going to use, don't mislead your recruits into thinking they will be involved in coming up with new ideas. If you are starting completely from scratch, on the other hand, let potential team members know that you want their assistance in brainstorming and deciding on a project. What tends to work best is to start somewhere between these two options. Your team members will be more engaged if they are given the opportunity to help think through what the fundraising activity will be. But if the process is too open-ended, they may come up with something you think is a bad idea and you'll be struck trying to figure out how to get them to move to something else while not alienating them in the process. You might want to recruit a few people, say three to five, to do the initial brainstorm and conceptualizing, where you decide between a series of house parties, a car wash, and a silent auction, for example, and then bring in a larger team for implementation and refining the activity further. It's also possible to find people who are willing to do one or two specific and time-limited activities without being part of the ongoing work of the core committee.

Be clear about how much time you're asking volunteers to commit to. If you want someone to sell raffle tickets, suggest how many you'd like them to sell. They can always say, "I can't sell that many, but I'll sell fewer." If you want a several-month commitment to organize an evening of jazz performed by local artists that also includes mounting a silent auction and producing an ad book, your team of volunteers needs to know what they're getting themselves into!

Resource A, the Volunteer Recruitment Form, can help you identify potential volunteers for your fundraising project. Use it to help brainstorm a list of potential candidates, then think about what it is you're asking them to do. Careful planning of your recruitment process will help you put together a strong and enthusiastic team.

You will have the most success recruiting people who know you or know the organization or project you're raising money for and who believe in the cause. If you're part of a larger organization, you'll want to ask staff members, board members, volunteers, active members, and donors.

To calculate how many people you need to ask to get the number of volunteers you actually need, figure that about 25 percent of the people you ask will ultimately show up. About half the people you ask will agree to volunteer, but only about half of them will follow through on what they said they would do. You may have a better response than this, but it's best to plan conservatively.

WORKING WITH A TEAM

Even if your activity won't require lots of meetings (which will make some people very happy), start off with at least one face-to-face gathering. This begins the process of relationship building that will ultimately help people work together more smoothly and make the experience a positive one.

Once you (or the team members) have settled on what the fundraising activity will be, the team will need to come up with a plan and a timeline. Each strategy outlined in this book provides instructions that will help you create a realistic timeline and that tell you how many people are needed to carry out the strategy successfully. The timeline and set of tasks within that timeline are important not just because they help make the activity be as successful as possible in reaching its goal, but also because they give members of the team a clear picture of what it will take so they can see how they may want to be involved.

Once the plan is complete, give the team members an opportunity to indicate how they want to help. Make sure they understand what kind of time commitment they're making and what the important deadlines are. This level of structure and detail is important with volunteers. Most people have many commitments and things in their lives that they need to stay on top of—job, family, and household responsibilities as well as other organizations or community projects they may be involved in. When team members are completely clear about what they've agreed to do for your fundraising project, it is much easier for them to be successful and for you to hold them accountable to that commitment.

An important step at the outset is finding out if the team needs any training on tasks they'll be working on. For example, if asking for money is something new or scary to members of the team, make sure you provide some training and coaching on how to do it. Selling ads to local businesses or soliciting auction items or prizes for a raffle may also be something people haven't done before, so be sure to give them some helpful "how-tos" and support them as they venture into the great unknown. At this session, which should take from two to three hours, volunteers should have a chance to talk about any anxieties they may have asking for money, learn some skills to make them more comfortable doing so, and complete their lists of people they will ask. Use the sample agenda that follows to plan your orientation and training session.

SAMPLE AGENDA FOR A TWO-HOUR ORIENTATION AND TRAINING SESSION

- Welcome and introductions; people share why they've agreed to participate in this fundraising project.

- Discuss the goals and process of the campaign: how much money you want to raise, what the money is for, what the best strategies might be for raising the money. Here's where you can solicit input from the group about what kind of activity they want to participate in.

- Have a discussion about people's fears and anxieties about asking for money (or in-kind gifts). Explain that a lot of people are reluctant to ask, but that most people give money away to causes they care about and that, by asking them for money, you're giving them the opportunity to be part of this exciting project, cause, or issue.

- Do a brief presentation on the process of asking, whether for money, an in-kind contribution for a raffle or auction, or to invite someone to attend a community dinner.

- Conduct role plays so that people can practice asking.

- Put together lists of people to ask.

You will also find training agendas tailored to the specific strategy you've chosen in the chapters for each of the following strategies: the personal ask (Chapter Five), phonebanks (Chapter Six), door-to-door fundraising (Chapter Seven), and ad books (Chapter Twelve).

TIPS ON BUILDING A STRONG FUNDRAISING TEAM

Here are a number of things you can do to help build a strong and enthusiastic fundraising team.

- Provide material support (background on what you're raising money for, sample letters to write, phone scripts for making follow-up calls, and so forth).

- Provide encouragement.

- Be a cheerleader, even when you don't feel like it.

- Show appreciation.

- If you're following up with someone who hasn't done what they said they would, be as specific as possible in your interactions with them. For example, rather than saying, "What's going on? I haven't heard from you in a while," say, "At the last meeting, you agreed to talk to five merchants from the local mall. I was wondering if you'd had a chance to do that yet."

- Allow for time during meetings for the team members to discuss how things are going and to give and get feedback from the group. Because things happen that you can't anticipate, you may need to make changes along the way. Let people know that there needs to be a certain amount of flexibility in order to function well as a group.

- Provide opportunities for team members to develop relationships with each other.

- Don't let all the work fall to one or two people. This leads to resentment and burn-out for those people and accusations of "control freak" and "know-it-all" from those who weren't doing the work. (If all the work is being done by one or two people, some people are not doing their share and others are willing to do more than their share. In other words, this is a dynamic.) People don't volunteer not because they are lazy but because they may have never done such a task before and don't feel confident in how to do it. Always explain briefly what is involved in each task. Offer to help or walk the person through the task ahead of time. The iron rule of organizing, according to the great organizer Saul Alinsky, is "Never do for someone what they could do for themselves."

- Don't keep people on the committee who aren't doing anything. If you do everything recommended here and you still have people who aren't working, take them aside privately and describe to them what they haven't done. "Sarah, you haven't taken on any tasks so far. Are there tasks you would like to do?" If Sarah says, "I plan to be involved in laying out the ad book," or "I thought I could be most useful in making follow-up calls," that's great; she clearly has a specific plan. However, if she says something like, "I've just been so busy," or "My cat got an infected tooth and giving him his medicine is just taking a lot of time," then you may want to offer them an exit: "If this committee is too much work for you right now, just let me know. I don't want you to feel obligated to stay on." Usually a person who is not doing their share will own up to it, and then together you can figure out whether the person should stop being part of the committee or whether that person has something that is useful to do. The ideal scenario is always to use everyone who wants to be involved.

- Use what works for you and your group. Each leader has different styles—just keep in mind the needs and styles of the rest of your group.

- Whereas some people are perfectly happy to take on a task they can do completely on their own, late at night at their computer, make sure that you also have opportunities for people to be engaged with each other, having some fun while doing something productive and socially responsible. Exhibit 2.1 presents some ideas for going beyond building a strong team to making fundraising fun for the team.

GIVING FEEDBACK TO VOLUNTEERS

The time that volunteers will need the most encouragement and feedback is when they're in the process of soliciting pledges, auction items, or just cash for the cause. If you find that someone needs some constructive criticism on their approach to potential supporters, it's most useful to do it as a "praise sandwich"—that is, start with praise, give feedback on where they could do better, and end with praise. Be as specific as possible so that your praise seems sincere and so that your critiques are constructive, and give people specific suggestions on how to improve. For example, when giving someone feedback at a phonebank, "Oh you are great!" doesn't help someone as much as "Wow, I really liked how friendly and conversational you

Exhibit 2.1
Ideas for Making Fundraising Fun for Your Team

Try some of the following:

• Begin each meeting reminding people why you are doing this work—or better yet, ask them to say something about why they're involved.

• Do simple icebreakers so people get to know each other better.

• At some meetings, bring some treats and hand each member of the team one while thanking them for something they have done since the last meeting.

• Provide food, especially if meetings take place during a mealtime.

• Send a quick e-mail to people who complete their tasks: "Jody—good job with the printer!"

• Give members of your team chances to compliment and encourage each other. Pair people up to do things like soliciting ads for an ad book, doing door-to-door fundraising, soliciting auction items.

• Start the meeting by having each person say one thing that is going well and one thing they feel frustrated about with regard to the activity. People are often critical of themselves; this is a time to reassure people if you think they actually are doing a good job and to brainstorm with the group if a job is not getting done.

• Give out prizes to people for various achievements: raised the most money, got the largest number of donations, endured the worst refusal. The purpose of the prizes is not to make people feel bad or create negative competition, but to create a fun atmosphere.

• Have visuals such as thermometers or chart paper to give people a sense of their goals and accomplishments.

• Have a sense of humor.

were. You are great at connecting with people. Can I make a quick suggestion, too? I noticed that you chatted with the person a long time, and then they had to hang up before you got to ask them for money. Maybe next time you could be clear with them earlier in the call that you are making fundraising calls and then jump into engaging them about our project. You have a knack for making our project sound very dynamic."

ADDRESSING COMMON TEAM PROBLEMS

There are a few problems that seem to come up with most teams: personality conflicts, things getting bogged down, or a team leader who seems to take over rather than lead. Here are some ideas for how to handle these situations.

Personality conflicts. Try to separate the people who are in conflict and have them not work with each other at all. From time to time remind people that you are working as a team for a specific, time-limited project. You are not making a lifelong commitment to one another. You are not going into business together. All you have to do is get along for this short period of time.

Things get bogged down. Figure out one thing you can do to jumpstart the process. For example, if no one is making their follow-up calls, have everyone get out their cell phones and make one call during the meeting. If the event is getting too complicated, take one element out. One small organization wanted to do a dinner dance with both a silent auction and a live auction. When they realized the plan required far too much work and too many logistics, they discussed what would be the most fun and then eliminated both the auctions. With much enthusiasm, they then focused on the dinner and dancing.

The team leader is controlling and second-guesses everyone's work. We always say in fundraising, "If all else fails, try honesty." It also helps to assume good intent, even if a person's behavior leads you to think otherwise. Although many people find it difficult to confront someone who is making life miserable for everyone involved, the alternative is that people stop participating, especially if they are volunteers. It's worth taking the risk to bring up the problem directly and let the person know how their behavior affects you. Be specific and as nonjudgmental as possible. Address this early on in the process before you are so angry that you can't have a reasonable conversation.

AFTER THE PROJECT IS COMPLETED: EVALUATION AND APPRECIATION

Often the aftermath of a major undertaking like this is a kind of letdown. The team has spent a lot of time making something happen, often more time than they initially expected or thought they had signed on for, and even when the outcome is extremely positive people can have a feeling of anticlimax. Or, if the event was challenging, people may want to throw in the towel and never show up again to work on your project. Two steps at this phase of the project can help people leave feeling good about what they've done.

The first step is to schedule a final meeting of the entire team to do an evaluation of the project and to make any recommendations for future efforts. If the activity was a one-time-only event, this can still be a useful way to give some closure to everyone involved. Here is a sample agenda for such a closing meeting.

WRAP-UP MEETING AGENDA

First, report on the results of the activity:

- How much money was raised.
- How many people participated, either by giving money, buying tickets, or in other ways. (This is actually a much more important number than how much money was raised. If one person gave you $2,000 or one hundred people gave gifts of $10 to $250 that totaled $2,000, this tells you a lot more about what happened than just the fact that you raised $2,000.)
- How many people helped out as volunteers.
- Other possible outcomes, such as coverage in the local newspaper or radio station, or connections made to people who can be helpful to the project or organization in the future.
- New skills learned.
- Will we do this again next year?
- What else?

Then, have some questions for the group to discuss to bring in their assessment of the project. Here are some examples:

- What do you think went well with this fundraising activity?

- What didn't go well?

- What did you most enjoy about working on this fundraising activity?

- What was most difficult or challenging for you?

- How well did you feel the team worked together? What feedback would you give to the people who coordinated or oversaw the process of organizing this activity?

- What do you think could be done differently in the future to make the activity more successful, more fun to work on, and better able to recruit more people to help out?

- Would you participate in an activity like this in the future?

COORDINATOR'S TIPS

As a coordinator, you may find yourself helping to coordinate an activity that you have limited or no more experience doing than the rest of the team. Don't worry! That's how we all learn. Find the balance between being honest with the team that you are learning as well and sabotaging yourself by discrediting your ability to take leadership and help coordinate anyway. If you have done the activity once yourself, you may also build up the confidence to train others. For example, if you are coordinating a raffle, go out and sell tickets yourself so that you can speak from experience about what works and what doesn't. If you are coordinating a phonebank, take a list and make several calls yourself so you can get comfortable with what you say and so that you can test out to see if the materials you've prepared work.

Often other members of your team, like you, are nervous about fundraising or getting the specific strategy right. Being well organized with your materials and conveying some faith and confidence in your team will go a long way toward making your team feel confident enough to do the job.

By building a strong volunteer team, your fundraising efforts will be much more effective, you will develop your team's skills, and you'll have much more fun in the process!

The Importance of "Thank-You"

Whatever strategy or combination of strategies you decide to use, common to all fundraising, whether for a one-time need or something ongoing, is thanking people for their support. This includes thanking not only the people who made a contribution of money, but also those who donated their time. (Exceptions might be people who come to your car wash, or buy a $1 raffle ticket.) Thanking people is important for a number of reasons:

- People like to feel appreciated. All of us like to know that our contributions are really helpful, make a difference, and are at least *noticed* by those we're giving to.

- People want to know that their contribution actually arrived. A cancelled check or credit card bill will eventually tell them you received the donation, but sometimes that takes a while, and people often worry that their check got lost.

- Because of the number of scandals in the nonprofit sector that have been widely publicized in the past several years, people also worry that their money has been misused. A follow-up thank-you note, while no real guarantee that the money has been spent properly, gives people some reassurance that it probably has.

- A thank-you strengthens your relationship with your supporters and helps them feel good about you and the project.

- If there's any chance you will be going back to your supporters to ask for their help again, whether to repeat your effort on an annual basis or for something completely different down the road, you will have a much better chance of getting someone to give time or money again if you thank them the first time around.

So, the very first thing you do, within a week after your fundraising project is wrapped up, is send out thank-you notes to everyone who gave and to everyone who volunteered to make it happen. Here are few things to remember in writing thank-yous:

- Be sure to thank the donor for exactly what they gave or the volunteer for exactly what they did, such as, "Thank you for your gift of $35," or "Thank you for your donation of one copy of your wonderful book, *Gardening for the Left Handed,*" or "Thank you for all the time you put into helping organize the auction. I know we couldn't have done it without you."

- While it is unlikely you would write a thank-you note to someone who bought an item at an auction, garage sale, or the like, if you do acknowledge such a gift, let the donor know that their gift is not tax deductible. If part of their gift is, in fact, tax deductible, such as a dinner at a restaurant that normally costs $20 but for which the donor paid $40, let them know that only the amount that is greater than the market value of the gift is tax deductible, in this case the $20 beyond the value of the meal. Check with your local nonprofit assistance center, volunteer center, or even a larger nonprofit if you are uncertain about the exact tax deductibility of any gift.

- When nothing of material value has been given to the donor, include this sentence in your thank-you letter: "No goods or services have been exchanged for your gift."

- You are required to provide a receipt for any tax-deductible gift of more than $250. A thank-you note specifying the amount given serves as a receipt.

- If possible, tell the donor the total you brought in from your fundraising effort: "As you may remember, we needed $5,000 to bring the electrical system in our community center up to code. Thanks to you and one hundred other people, our campaign has already netted $4,500."

The best thank yous are handwritten (but legible). If you have a manageable number of donors, this is not difficult. Ask volunteers to help write them.

Here are some sample thank-yous:

Dear Natalia,

Thank you so much for your gift of $35 to help us fight the anti-gay ballot initiative that is coming up for a vote this November. Your support means a lot to us, and not just financially. Your gift lets us know that there are people in our community who are as angry as we are about this initiative and who are willing to speak out and make a difference. To keep posted on how this work is going, log on to www.equalmeasure.org.

Thanks again,

(Your Name)

Dear Francisco,

When we started our campaign to raise $5,000 to get our bookmobile, people told us there weren't enough people with money in our small town to support this project. Your participation in our bowlathon, for which you brought in $250 in pledges, was a great boost to the campaign. We raised a total of $1,300 from that event, and with the other activities we have planned, we are confident that we'll reach our goal by the end of this year. Thank you for being part of this community effort. The success of this campaign showed us that if people are really committed to something, we are unstoppable!

All the best,

(Your Name)

Another way to thank and acknowledge people for their support is to make it public. Here are a few ways to do that:

- If you have a newsletter or other regular way you keep in touch with people, include an appreciation page in one issue on which you name everyone that helped out, financially and with their time.

- If your community has a local newspaper that covers lots of community events and news, ask them to publish a short piece that describes your project and how you were able to raise money for it and that mentions the fact that a lot of people came forward to make it a success. If you have photos of an event, a local paper may be willing to include one. This is not as personal for your supporters, of course, but those who were part of the effort will feel proud to see the event in print.

- For an activity in which you're raising money in advance of an event from sponsors, advertisers, and others, make sure you list their names in your program or ad book.

Of all the tasks related to fundraising, sending thank-you notes has to be the easiest, and yet often it is the most neglected. Make a point to send simple notes to everyone who supports you. People will notice, appreciate it, and be more likely to give again.

Beyond One-Time Fundraising

This book is written for people who are raising money for a one-time, short-term project and who don't plan on building an ongoing fundraising program. But many things can happen that turn your one-time effort into a longer-term commitment.

Here's an example:

> A community that prided itself on a thriving downtown with many independent businesses and few chain stores was approached by a big, discount "box store" that wanted to open a store a few miles outside of town. With its lower prices and much-publicized free parking, this store would have likely drawn business from several of the downtown businesses. A small group of community residents got together to fight the opening of the store. With much effort, they enlisted the support of the majority of the town's residents in a campaign to get the city council to deny approval to the store. They raised money from community members to pay a community organizer for the year-long campaign. They kept track of everyone who was involved—those who gave money, helped raise money, or helped out in other ways. Several months after winning the box-store battle, the community learned that a luxury housing development was being considered that would displace low-income residents. With their list of supporters and volunteers who had worked on the box-store campaign, they could quickly gear up to stop the luxury housing development.

You might discover after engaging in an exciting fundraising activity that the need you're raising money for is actually larger and longer-term than you initially thought or that you really enjoyed raising money and are ready to commit to continuing the effort.

If you're raising money to organize a one-time conference, rehabilitate a historic building, or send emergency aid to a community that just survived a natural disaster, you don't need to pay as much attention to infrastructure and record keeping. But with the awareness that you never know what needs or opportunities for mobilizing people to action may present themselves down the road, including fundraising action, here are some things to plan for so that you or others can continue raising money for whatever cause may arise.

RECORD KEEPING

The key to a successful ongoing fundraising program is keeping track of what you do and who is involved in helping you. If you want people to give you not just one gift one time but to contribute once a year or even several times a year over several years, you need to know when and how much they gave and in response to what appeal or circumstance.

If you leave the project, a new person should be able to look at your database and paper files and start in where you left off.

There is nothing more alienating to your supporters than getting a letter or call asking for a contribution that doesn't acknowledge their prior relationship with the organization. This type of oversight is more common than you might think. To help you avoid making that mistake, Worksheet 4.1 provides a simple form for keeping track of everyone who made a donation. If you are keeping track of donations on a computer, you can use a simple database program or a spreadsheet in the beginning. If you decide you will be doing fundraising in a long-term, ongoing way, you will want to graduate to a database specifically designed for fundraising. We recommend that you purchase an inexpensive, off-the-shelf program, which you can find for about $100, to start, then move on to more powerful—and more expensive—programs as your fundraising program—and your budget to build it—grows.

DOCUMENTING WHAT HAPPENED

In order to learn from what went well and what didn't, document how you accomplished your project. Imagine that a year from now, someone else wants to try organizing a dinner, an auction, or a phonebank. They can read this book, but even

Worksheet 4.1
Sample Form for Tracking Donors

Name	Address	Phone	E-mail	Amount donated	Date of donation	Fundraising strategy	Comments	Date thanked
Jill Chan				$50	8/12/04	Phonebank	Former board member	9/5/04
Kyle Davis				$25	8/12/04	Phonebank	Prefers e-mail contact	9/5/04
Josie Sanchez				$100	11/2/04	House party	Long-time supporter	11/22/04
Craig Yoshikawa				$50	3/10/05	Annual dinner	Don't phone	3/18/05
Sara Nelson				$250	3/10/05	Annual dinner	Former volunteer, Sam's partner	3/18/05

better will be the actual experience that you had, including how much it cost, who volunteered, who is likely to be willing to volunteer again, how much money you raised, and so forth. Write down what happened, what took more time than you expected, any changes in the workplan that you would want to implement next time, and anything else that would be useful to someone else who wants to try out this fundraising activity.

RELATIONSHIP BUILDING AND COMMUNITY BUILDING

Fundraising is about much more than getting money to do the things you want to do. It's also about building awareness in the community about community issues and problems, mobilizing people to *do* something (including but not limited to giving money), and giving people a way to take action as part of a larger group in order to have an impact that they couldn't have as individuals acting alone.

Fundraising is ultimately about making a difference in the world. By consciously seeking to build closer ties to your supporters and all of the people who are involved in furthering the work, you will develop the kinds of relationships with people that will have lasting and continued impact. As fundraising trainer Kim Klein says in her article in the *Grassroots Fundraising Journal,* "The Fine Art of Asking for the Gift," "Many people have discovered that doing face-to-face fundraising reminds them of the true depth of their commitment to an organization. They remember why they became involved with the work in the first place and why they think the work is important."

When MoveOn.org asked all their supporters in spring 2004 to hold a bake sale on the same day to raise funds to fight the reelection of President Bush, one thousand bake sales took place around the country. The bake sales were not only a fundraising activity, they were, more important, a public relations opportunity that let thousands of people all over the country know that there was a grassroots groundswell of opposition to President Bush's reelection.

Ultimately, it's not just the money you raise, but the coming together of people who share a vision, a set of beliefs, and the willingness to take action toward a common goal that will lead to success, whatever your cause.

LEADERSHIP DEVELOPMENT

The term *leadership development* means different things to different people. It has come to encompass everything from community organizing to youth empowerment to skill-building in a range of areas. To some it means board development, running effective meetings and managing conflict in a group. In this chapter, leadership development means continually looking for ways to develop skills among a broad group of people in order to develop an ongoing and successful fundraising program that grows and raises more money every year. Even if you're doing a one-time bowlathon for a specific purpose, every chance you have to give the people involved more responsibility increases the chance they'll take the lead in the next fundraising project. Because even the *idea* of fundraising scares off so many people, it is that much more important to create a plan for involving more people in the work and providing opportunities for people to learn the skills they need in order to participate effectively.

How do you do this? Here are some suggestions:

- Make the experience of raising money a positive one. Encourage people to do things they are most comfortable with initially, then build up to things they feel less sure of.

- Make sure you have enough people, lead time, and upfront funds to implement a given fundraising activity successfully. Rather than hold that dreamed-of gala with a famous entertainer—which requires a large number of volunteers, up to a year of lead time, a *real* connection to the entertainer, and a fair amount of front money—consider starting with something that fits better with the scale of your group's resources and likelihood of success.

- Find ways for people to learn new skills: bring in a trainer, send people to workshops, do role playing and practice sessions in the group.

- Don't assume that the best person for any given task is the person who has always done it. Encourage people to try new things, and provide ways for them to get support in doing so.

- Identify people whom you think would be good for a specific task or committee and invite them personally to get involved. When someone calls Maria and says, "Maria, I think you'd be a great member of this committee. You have great people skills, and because you've lived in this community so long and know all of the merchants on Main Street, you'd probably be able to get more raffle prizes donated than anyone else," you can be sure she'll feel flattered and interested in helping if she can.

- Invite feedback after a fundraising activity is completed, with a commitment to incorporate useful ideas the next time around. Identify what went well and don't get defensive if people have a number of ideas of how things could have been better. See it as a sign of their ownership and enthusiasm.

- Be scrupulous and transparent about all finances. This is important not only because you want to be responsible about how you raise and use money, but also because people will take on greater responsibility in groups if they understand what it costs to do the work and how the money they're raising is being spent.

All of the strategies are designed to stand on their own, but we hope that as you try them out, you will raise money, gain skills, enjoy the process, and consider making fundraising a more ongoing part of your work!

PART TWO

Fundraising Strategies

The following chapters describe in detail how to implement eleven different fundraising strategies. Before deciding on which strategy suits you best, read through each chapter to understand the elements that will make that activity successful, the time required to carry it out, and the ideal number of people needed on your team.

The strategies are grouped under three distinct types of activities. The first set of strategies involves *asking people* directly for a contribution. There is no event the donors attend or product they receive in return for their gift. While these are probably the most challenging strategies to implement because they require you to feel comfortable asking for money for your cause, they also tend to generate the most money for the time involved in carrying them out. The second set of strategies, *social gatherings,* focuses on activities that bring people together—at someone's home, in a larger public setting, or to carry out a pledge-raising event, better known as some kind of "thon" (such as a walkathon). These are probably the most common fundraising activities the world over and can be a lot of fun. Because of all the details involved in making them successful, they need to be planned carefully and engage a reliable team of volunteers to avoid being a lot of work for little financial return. Finally, the activities described in the four chapters that involve *selling* generally work because the donor is getting something tangible from the transaction. It may be publicity for their business (ad book), a clean car (car wash), a chance at a prize (raffle), or inexpensive second-hand goods (garage sale). For the most part (other than the ad book), they are events that most pe[o]ple familiar with and may have experience doing in other settings. As hard to find a few people to help carry them out, and th without a lot of lead time.

Each strategy is accompanied by a real-life example of how a group was able to accomplish it with an all or mostly volunteer team. We hope these stories will inspire you by their creativity and, in some cases, fun new twists on an old idea.

Every strategy in this book is one that a committed group of volunteers can successfully carry out, and each one comes with its own sets of benefits and challenges. Take the time to consider what your fundraising goals are, which strategy is most likely to work in your community, and which of them will bring you the results you're seeking. Don't be tempted to choose a strategy simply because you've heard of it or because you're afraid to take a risk with another one—that one might actually benefit your cause more in the long run. The strategy that will work the best is the one that you are confident in doing.

Asking People

The Personal Ask

If we were to choose one strategy that is the simplest, most straightforward, and most likely to get you the money you need right *now,* asking someone directly (one-on-one) would get our vote. It doesn't require huge amounts of preparation, the costs are minimal, and it can be done very quickly. Basically, this strategy involves coming up with a list of people you know who you think might be willing to give money to your project and then asking them for a contribution. There's no gimmick, nothing the donor gets back other than a thank-you note and the good feeling that they've helped support something or someone they care about. In order to be successful, the strategy requires you to come up with a list of people to ask and a willingness to ask them.

BEST USES

Personal asking is an ideal choice when you need to raise money in a hurry and if the issue you're raising money for is time specific and urgent. For example, people usually respond quickly and with great generosity to disaster-relief efforts because of the urgent and immediate need. Political elections, too, especially highly contested ones, will often generate donations from people who have strong feelings about one side or the other. However, asking people directly for financial support can be a successful strategy with *any* cause or within any time frame as long as you are willing to ask!

Personal asking is a great strategy if you know a lot of people whom you're willing to approach personally without offering them something concrete back. This is what differentiates this strategy from events, raffles, auctions, and so on. If you're comfortable asking people directly for money, you will have no problem carrying out the other strategies described in this book, where you will be asking for donations of goods and services as well as for time from volunteers. This strategy also can help deepen relationships with people who give because you're taking the time to speak with them directly, share why you're raising money, and hear what they think about your cause. If you want to do fundraising beyond a one-time ask, you will be able to build on these relationships, engage the people who give money, and ask them for a contribution in the future.

THINGS TO CONSIDER

While you can carry out this fundraising strategy by yourself, you'll obviously raise more money if you can recruit a few others to join you in the effort. Plan that each volunteer you recruit will be willing to ask about twenty of their friends (and neighbors, family, and so on). With a team of five people, you should be able to raise at least $1,000 in just a few weeks.

Finding a team of people to help do personal asking might be a greater challenge than for other strategies that have some other elements besides asking for money. This is why it is important to have elements of fun for your volunteers built into the direct ask strategy, such as an interactive training to kick off your direct asks or prizes for people who raise the most money.

COSTS

The costs of doing a one- or two-month individual donor drive are minimal. They include the following:

- Stamps for mailing letters
- Printing or photocopying a response card
- Envelopes (for sending the letter, and return envelopes for people to send back their contribution)
- Long-distance phone calls (if your list includes people far away)

MATERIALS NEEDED FOR VOLUNTEERS

It will be helpful to give volunteers copies of Resource B, Who Can You Ask?, to jog people's minds about their contacts and Resource C, Tips on Asking Individuals for Money. In addition are the following materials that are described further in the rest of this chapter.

- Sample letter (or preprinted letter with space for handwritten note)
- Response cards
- Envelopes (to mail letter in, plus return envelopes)
- Fact sheet or brief description of project
- Gift-range chart

STEPS TO TAKE

These are the steps you should plan on taking. Each will be discussed in detail.

1. Make a plan
2. Recruit volunteers
3. Make list of people to ask for money
4. Draft a sample letter and response form
5. Conduct a training and orientation session for volunteers
6. Send letters
7. Make follow-up phone calls
8. Send thank-you notes to donors
9. Evaluate the effort and thank volunteers

Step 1: Make a Plan

The planning process will help you set a goal for how much money you want to raise, figure out how many volunteers you need in order to carry out this strategy, and decide if your goals are realistic.

As you start putting your plan together, keep in mind that, because half the people you ask for a donation will say no, you need to ask two to three times as many people for a gift as will ultimately give you one. Also plan that people will give different amounts of money. Your temptation will be to think, "If I need $5,000 and I can get fifty people to give $100 each, I'll reach my goal." This calculation would be entirely accurate. However, years of fundraising experience have shown that if you ask a cross section of people to give the same dollar amount (say, $100), you will lose many contributions from people who would give *something*, but can't afford $100; on the other end of the spectrum, you will get $100 from people who would be willing and able to give much more. So, if you are trying to raise $5,000, you should plan to get a few contributions of $250 to $500, a few more between $100 and $250, and lots of contributions of $50 or less. Putting these numbers together into a planning tool called a gift-range chart will help you figure out how many contributions you'll need of what amounts in order to reach your goal.

It is also important to give your potential donors a clear idea of what you want from them. Just saying, "Give and be as generous as you can" is too vague and leaves people with the uneasy feeling that they don't know how much is generous enough or even how much you need. The gift-range chart described below will help you determine the amounts of money you need so you can think about who might be able to give at the different levels.

In order to create a gift-range chart, start with your fundraising goal (for example, $5,000). The largest gift you'll be seeking is one that equals 10 percent of the goal (in this example, $500). You want to try to get two gifts at that top level, or 20 percent of your goal from the amount raised at this level. The total amount you want to raise at the next-largest gift level should also equal 20 percent. You'll need more gifts at that level to reach that goal. Continue constructing your chart, so that the number of gifts you expect to receive at each level *increases* as the dollar amount of each level *decreases*.

In the *Grassroots Fundraising Journal*'s booklet *Getting Major Gifts*, Kim Klein warns not to become too concerned about the gift-range chart:

> Don't get too bogged down in making your gift-range chart. There is no scientific way to do it. Basically, the chart is a triangle with fewer people at the top and more people at the bottom. (In a rural, less populated area, you might need to have even larger gifts from even fewer people.) The point of the chart is to recognize that not everyone will give the same amount and to set a limit on the number of people needing to be solicited. Prospects and donors like this kind of plan because it lets them know that the group has planned its campaign and knows what it is doing.

Table 5.1 gives an example of the range of contributions you're likely to receive. You'll see that you will need a total of seventy contributions of varying amounts to reach your goal of $5,000. That means you need about 140 people to ask in order to make sure you'll reach your goal. You can see from this example that if you can

Table 5.1
Gift-Range Chart

| | | $5,000 Goal | |
Number of gifts	Amount	Number of people you need to ask	Total
2	$500	6	$1,000
4	$250	8–12	$1,000
12	$100	24	$1,200
20	$ 50	40	$1,000
32	$ 25	64	$ 800
70		~140	$5,000

get a group of five friends together and they each ask their friends, each of you will need to come up with between twenty-five and thirty names.

Step 2: Recruit Volunteers

This is one of the few strategies in this book that you *can* do by yourself, but it won't be as much fun and you won't raise as much money as you will if more people are involved. Use Resource A, Volunteer Recruitment Form, to help you come up with the names of potential volunteers. Here are the things you'll be recruiting people to do:

- Draft a sample letter asking for money
- Design and make copies of a response card
- Send letters to people they know
- Make follow-up phone calls

Not everyone on the team has to do everything. You need to have at least a few people who are willing to send a fundraising letter out to their friends, but even if someone really doesn't want to do that, they can help write the letter or send out the mailing.

Step 3: Make List of People to Ask for Money

After finding volunteers to help you carry out this fundraising activity, the key to success is coming up with a list of people to ask for money. Your first task as a committee, then, is for each member to come up with as many names as possible. A good time for this to occur is during the initial meeting and training of volunteers (see Step 5). Use Resource B, "Who Can You Ask?" for ideas on whom to put on your list. Each volunteer can put their names on their copy of Worksheet 5.1.

Once you've brainstormed names of everyone you know, have each volunteer use Worksheet 5.1 to identify the following information about each person:

- What is your relationship to them (and how strong is the relationship)?

- Are they likely to believe in this project (or at least not be opposed to it)?

- Are they donors to your group already, or to similar groups or causes?

The people most likely to give money from the lists compiled are those you know well, who care about the cause and who are people who give money away, as evidenced by being members or donors to other groups or belonging to a house of worship. Start with them.

Step 4: Draft a Sample Letter and a Response Form

It will speed up the process of getting everyone to send letters and make their "asks" if you provide a sample letter they can use or adapt. Also, provide the response form and return envelopes—having these sent with the letter helps increase the response rate. Asking for money can certainly be done by e-mail, and it works best with people askers are used to communicating with in this way. However, with e-mail, you can't include a return envelope—though you can attach a form that the recipient can download, print out, and send in with their contribution. For groups that have a Web site and the technology and financial systems that allow them to accept donations by credit card, you can include a link in an e-mail message that people can click on to go directly to the Web site and make a contribution by credit card. Use the medium that you think will work best for you and the people you are asking for money. Exhibit 5.1 shows the pros and cons of each option.

See Handout 5.1 for things to keep in mind while drafting your letter.

Worksheet 5.1
Potential Supporters

Use this form to create your list of people to ask for a donation. Refer to Resource B, "Who Can You Ask?" to help you come up with ideas that may not have occurred to you. Once you've created your list, decide how much money you'll request from each person. If you have absolutely no idea, then suggest a range, such as $25–$100.

Name and contact info	Relationship to you	Cares about cause?	Gives away money?	How much to ask for
Yolanda Johnson Address City, State, ZIP Phone and e-mail	Sister	Yes	Yes	$100
Brian Park Address City, State, ZIP Phone and e-mail	Neighbor	Not sure	Not sure, but he's a member of local church	$15–$25

Exhibit 5.1
Whether to Send by Postal Mail or E-Mail

Postal Mail	E-mail
+ Can send reply card and return envelope	+ Quick communication and ability to respond. People can make pledge by e-mail and follow up with sending check.
+ Can write personal note, add personal touch	
+ May stand out more (since personal mail is more rare these days)	+ If this is a good way to communicate with your network, use it!
	+ If you have a Web site where people can make donations, you can add the link to your e-mail.
+ Can send newspaper clips, use graphics	
− Stamps and paper cost money	+ If you have the know-how, you can send newspaper clips and use graphics.
− Takes longer to get mailing out	
	− Can't send reply envelope (but you can make a reply form for people to print)

Here are some sample letters:

TO CONTINUE A SCHOOL MUSIC PROGRAM

Dear Friends and Family,

I think you know how much our kids love the music classes they've taken in school, including the opportunity to perform with the choir every year. What you may not know is that as a result of the recent state cuts in education funding, all music instruction will be eliminated starting in the fall. Many of the parents are getting together to see what we can do to get the funding reinstated. In the meantime, we're trying to raise $20,000 to keep at least one part-time music teacher on staff for the next school year.

Handout 5.1
Tips on Writing the Letter

• *In simple, straightforward language, tell the reader what you're raising money for.* Telling a story about someone affected by the issue gets the reader's attention better than broad, sweeping statements. (See the sample letter about the earthquake in Honduras.)

• *Tell them what your relationship to the issue is.* The person you are asking has a relationship with you, so it helps them to see why you feel connected to the issue.

• *Be specific about what you want.* Telling your potential supporters how much money you need to raise and the size of contributions you're looking for gives them a way to think about what would be an appropriate amount to donate.

• *State in the letter that you will be calling them to follow up and discuss the request with them.* If you're asking for a gift of $500 or more, offer to meet with them in person to discuss the request.

A group of about twenty-five parents has come up with some ideas for how to raise the money. We decided that one thing we would do is ask some of our family, friends, and neighbors to help out.

I'm writing to you as someone who believes that education is about more than just "the basics," that it includes subjects like music and art. We understand that we cannot make up for the loss of government support for these programs, but we believe that if enough of us protest these cuts, the programs will be reinstated.

In the meantime, we're hoping that friends like you will consider making a contribution toward our goal of $20,000. Any amount will help—$10, $25, $100, or even more.

I'll give you a call within the next couple of weeks to talk more about this with you and to see if you have any questions. I've included an envelope and a form you can send back with your contribution.

I really appreciate your thinking about this request.

Sincerely,

TO SUPPORT DISASTER RELIEF EFFORTS IN AN IMMIGRANT COMMUNITY'S HOME COUNTRY

Dear Friends,

As you know, the recent earthquake in Honduras left our home town of San Pedro Sula totally devastated. In addition to the loss of many lives, the earthquake caused thousands of people to lose their homes. I am so thankful that my grandparents and cousins who still live there are all safe, but like so many, their home suffered a lot of damage. Until repairs are made they are staying with friends who live in a village nearby.

I'm writing to ask for your help. Our hometown association is trying to raise $15,000 to help repair and rebuild twenty homes in the town of San Pedro Sula. You would be surprised at how far that money will go and what a difference it will make for families that have nowhere to live right now.

I hope you can make a donation. We're looking for contributions of $5 to $500. Of course, any amount is greatly appreciated. I'll call you soon to see what you might be able to do.

Thank you,

TO SEND COMMUNITY MEMBERS TO A CONFERENCE

Dear Friends and Family,

I hope this letter finds all of you well and I apologize in advance that this is a form letter. Please take the time to read it anyway, and know that I will be calling each of you soon to follow up on my request.

As you know, last year a GLBT (Gay, Lesbian, Bisexual, Transgender) Community Center opened in a large room in the basement of the Quaker Meeting House here in our small town. Since it opened, more than twenty events have been held there, with more than one thousand people attending in all. Some people have driven more than four hours from their ranches and farms to attend. Our hotline receives ten or more calls a day, and we have recently opened a small GLBT library and "coffee shop" (basically a couch and chair near the sink, with a coffeepot). It is simple, but so important that GLBT people have a local place to call our own.

We have been invited to a conference called "Creating Change," which is sponsored by the National Gay and Lesbian Task Force in Washington, D.C., to talk about organizing a community center in a rural community. They have asked us to reflect on our struggles, how we publicize ourselves, and why we think we have been able to be so successful. We will be with other rural GLBT organizations, as well as more than two thousand other GLBT activists. The conference will pay for one person to go, but we see this as a great opportunity to meet other people and get more ideas for programs and services we can offer.

The conference is in Milwaukee this year, and we'd like to send four of our active members. Someone has offered to put us up, so the costs are for airfare, ground transportation, and meals. We estimate it will cost $2,000 for all of us to go. We are each approaching friends and family for donations toward this trip.

I am hoping you will help with a gift of any size—nothing is too large or too small. I am writing to twenty people and hoping to raise $500 or more. Gifts in the range of $25 to $100 will get me to my goal quickly.

I'll be calling you within the next couple of weeks to answer any questions you may have and to ask more personally for your support. Thank you in advance for helping me out with this.
Sincerely,

Exhibit 5.2 shows a sample reply card that can be sent with the letters. Notice that it gives a range of responses and also includes a place for someone to write in their own amount.

Exhibit 5.2
Sample Reply Card

Yes, I want to help the residents of San Pedro Sula rebuild their homes. Here is my contribution of:

$15_____ $25_____ $50_____ $100_____ $_____ (other)

_____Please keep me posted on your progress.

Name _____

Address _____

City, State, ZIP _____

E-mail _____

Phone _____

(Please make checks payable to San Pedro Sula Relief and send to 1234 Main Street, Our Town, IL 60000)

Step 5: Conduct a Training and Orientation Session for Volunteers

Because this strategy of asking individuals to give money is not done in a group, but one person at a time, there is little opportunity for the volunteers involved to feel they're connected to the larger effort. It is therefore important to bring everyone together at the beginning of the campaign to get clear instructions and some training on how to ask for money and to build the excitement of a team working together toward a common goal.

At this session, which should take from two to three hours, volunteers will have a chance to talk about any anxieties they may have asking for money, learn some skills to make them more comfortable asking, and complete their lists of people to ask.

SAMPLE AGENDA FOR THE ORIENTATION AND TRAINING SESSION:

1. Welcome and introductions. People share why they've agreed to participate in this fundraising project.

2. Discuss the goals and process of the campaign: how much money you want to raise, what the money is for, how long the campaign will last, approximately how many people will need to be asked for money.

3. Answer any questions people have about the campaign itself.

4. Have a discussion about people's fears and anxieties about asking for money. Give volunteers a chance to talk about their feelings. Explain that most people find asking for money challenging at first but that, with a little practice, they'll find it's not as scary as they think.

5. Do a brief presentation on the process of asking: people will send a letter or e-mail, follow up with a phone call, either ask for the contribution on the phone or ask to meet in person to discuss a contribution.

6. Conduct role plays so that people can practice making a phone call to ask someone for money.

7. Put together lists of people to ask.

8. If there's time, have people write personal notes on the letters at this meeting.

Step 6: Send Letters

Immediately after the training and orientation session, volunteers should complete and send their letters (or e-mails). Some groups find it easier to add another hour to the training and have everyone sign and add personal notes on the letters, which have been prepared ahead of time. This way, there is no delay in getting the letters in the mail. Personal notes are an important touch because it is the relationship with the people being asked that will be one of the main reasons the donors give.

Step 7: Make Follow-Up Phone Calls

One week after sending out the letters, each volunteer should call the people they sent letters to, asking if they have any questions and if they are willing to give money to the project. The follow-up call is one of the most important steps and is key to the success of this strategy. It is also the most difficult task for many people who are reluctant to solicit someone directly for a contribution. However, if your volunteers don't make these calls, far fewer people will send in a contribution. Expect that about 10 percent to 20 percent of the people who receive your letter will send in a donation without a follow-up call. You can easily double that response by calling. Often people need that call as a reminder to read your letter. Or they may have read it, put it aside to get to later, and then forgotten about it. People also appreciate the personal connection.

One thing to note, however, is to remind volunteers that since they are writing and calling their own personal network, it is helpful to make the purpose of the call clear at the beginning. Certainly, it is important and natural to chat and catch up with friends or family, but if they don't know right away that this call is to follow up on the fundraising letter, it may feel awkward to bring it up later in the conversation. It is also helpful to put the purpose of the call up front to have a clear focus to the conversation and not stray too far from the goal of sharing the project and asking them to help.

If there are people on a volunteer's list who he or she thinks could give $500 or more, the volunteer should offer to meet with them in person unless they live far away. In-person meetings are much more effective because people expect to spend more time in a face-to-face meeting than on the phone (though you don't need more than thirty minutes for the meeting), and both parties' taking the time to meet increases the chances that the prospect will make a contribution.

See Handout 5.2 for tips on making phone calls for personal asks.

Script 5.1 is a sample script for making follow-up calls after sending a fundraising letter. The basic structure outlined here can be adapted, depending on the issue you're raising money for and who you're talking to. Your volunteers should use this as a guideline, but emphasize that they should not read from a script but use their own words.

Use Worksheet 5.2 to keep track of your requests for support.

Tips on Making Phone Calls for Personal Asks

Here are some things to keep in mind as you begin to make your phone calls:

- Relax and be yourself—you're calling people who know and like you!

- Let the person know why you are calling near the beginning of the conversation.

- Assume support, be confident, and be as direct as possible ("We're working to win . . . ," not "We hope to get . . .").

- Use your own words. Don't read from a script.

- Listen; give people a chance to speak, ask a question, or voice an opinion about the issue.

- If someone asks you a question that you don't know the answer to, be honest and tell them you don't know. Let them know you'll get back to them (and then make a note of it and *do* get back to them yourself or make sure someone else does).

- Keep it short and simple. Be clear, concise, and direct.

- Ask for a specific amount of money.

- Once you make the ask, be silent (let them think about it and answer; don't fill the space with nervous chatter).

- Once they make a specific commitment, thank them and make sure they have what they need to send in a contribution. If they need to think about it, ask if there are any questions you can answer right now. If they still need to think, make a specific time to call them back (and then follow up).

- Thank them for their time.

- Remember that practice makes perfect!

Script 5.1
Sample Phone Script for Follow-Up Calls

Structure of what to say	What to say
Introduction—who you are, brief greeting, purpose of call	"Hi, this is Jody. How are you? As you may know from the letter I sent you recently, I've been active with the Honduras Relief Effort, and I'm calling to follow up on that letter. Do you have a couple of minutes right now?" (If they say no, they can't talk right now:) "When would be a better time? I'd be happy to call you back when it's more convenient." (If they have time, even a minute, continue.)
Explain problem and what you're raising money for; speak briefly about the project you're raising money for	"The letter I sent you a few days ago is about the recent earthquake in Honduras and the work some of us are doing to raise money to help with relief efforts. Did you get my letter?" (Wait for their answer. Continue if they're not sure what it was about:) "As you know, the earthquake last month caused not only millions of dollars' worth of damage, but also left a lot of people homeless. My hometown, San Pedro Sula, was devastated. I'm grateful that my grandparents and cousins who live there are safe, but their home was damaged. My hometown association is working to raise $15,000 to help build new housing and repair homes that were not completely demolished. I'm calling everyone I know to ask if they can donate some money for this cause."
Ask if they have questions	"Do you have any questions?" (Pause and wait for them to respond. Once you've answered their questions, continue:)
Ask for a contribution	"Your support would be such an incredible help to the residents of San Pedro Sula. Do you think you could give $50?" (At this point, stop and listen.)
If they say yes	"Thanks so much! What should I put you down for? Do you still have the form and envelope I included with my letter?" (If not, offer to send another one.)
If they say no	"Thank you for taking the time to talk to me. Can I come back to you another time?" (If they say they just can't afford to give right now, and you will be doing another fundraising campaign in the future, it's a good idea to ask if you can contact them again. If they really aren't interested in your project, just thank them and say goodbye.)
If they hesitate or seem unsure	(Ask if they have more questions or if they need time to think about it.)
Thank them!	"Thank you for taking the time to talk to me. I really appreciate it."

Worksheet 5.2
Tracking Form for Asks Made

Use this form to keep track of your requests for support. It's easy to forget who you called, when you left a message, and how much they said they'd give if you don't write it down.

Name of prospect	Date letter (or e-mail) sent	Date phone call(s) made	Result/notes	Amount pledged	Date $ received and amount	Date Thank you sent
Yolanda Johnson	10/12	10/20 10/24	left message	will give $50	11/15 $50	11/20
Brian Park	10/12	10/22 10/25 10/31	left message left message talked briefly	no, but maybe another time		

Step 8: Send Thank-You Notes to Donors

As soon as possible after you receive someone's contribution, write them a thank-you note. "Thank before you bank" is a good policy to follow and will make it more likely that you'll get thank-you notes out in a timely way. If you get your volunteers together for an evaluation, you could bring blank thank-you notes for people to write together.

If your project is ongoing or you know you'll want to carry out more fundraising activities in the future, keep track of everyone who gave and how much they donated, the date of their gift, and who knows them. Refer to Worksheet 4.1, Sample Form for Tracking Donors, in Chapter Four.

Step 9: Evaluate the Results and Thank Volunteers

When you are done with the project, come back together with your volunteers to evaluate your efforts. How much money did you raise collectively? How many people gave? Celebrate and recognize people's efforts. What worked? What would you do differently next time? Even if you did not meet your goals, what were lessons learned? You want people to have a good experience and to learn from this effort so that they will continue working on the project and so that they increase their enthusiasm for fundraising.

JEWISH YOUTH FOR COMMUNITY ACTION

Jewish Youth for Community Action is an organization based in Oakland, California, that develops the leadership skills of high-school-age Jewish youth as they become involved in social action and community projects. Because there is just one part-time paid staff person, fundraising activities are carried out by the youth and their parents. For the past two years they have written a fundraising letter that they send to their friends, family members, alumni of the program, and past donors to the project. The youth then make follow-up calls to everyone who received a letter. Last year they raised $5,000 from this strategy.

WORKPLAN

The following workplan provides a summary of the key steps necessary to implement this fundraising strategy and an estimated time frame for each step. It is meant to be a template from which to create your own plan and your own timeline. By taking the time to create a plan and timeline, you'll be more organized, more likely to avoid last-minute crises, and ultimately more successful in raising the money you need.

Workplan 5.1
The Personal Ask

What	Who	When (Week Number)									Done
		1	2	3	4	5	6	7	8	9	
1. Make a plan		x									
Create a gift-range chart		x									
2. Recruit volunteers		x									
3. Compile names of people to ask for $		x	x								
4. Prepare materials											
Sample letter, response form, envelopes			x								
5. Conduct training and orientation			x								
6. Send letters					x	x					
7. Make follow-up calls						x	x	x	x		
Meet with donors (for requests of $500+)							x	x	x	x	
Check in with volunteers						x	x	x			
8. Send thank you notes									x	x	
9. Evaluate										x	

Phonebanks

Phonebanking involves a group of people coming together in one place to call a large number of people for a specific reason—in this case, to raise money. The fundamental component of a phonebank is having a group of people making calls. If you have only a couple of people phoning, it's not a phonebank. Phonebanking as described in this chapter is a great way to reach a lot of people very quickly. The more people you have calling, the more people you'll reach. If you are trying to raise $5,000 from a list of five hundred people, it would take one person about seventeen hours of phoning to call them all. With ten people phoning, you could get through the list in an evening. Another advantage to a well-run phonebank is that it's a great way to deepen your relationships with the people making the calls. When someone comes in and raises money, they are likely to feel more connected to your group. Phonebanks can be fun if you create a supportive and enjoyable atmosphere. Cheer people on, feed them, talk up how important the goal is, and so on.

Of all the fundraising strategies that potential donors love to hate, telephone solicitations are on the top of the list. People associate these calls with telemarketing by credit card companies, long distance phone services, and the like. What will make people respond more favorably to your phonebank is that they are familiar with either the person making the call or the cause they're being asked to give to. People also tend to respond better if they know that the caller is a volunteer, as a person taking their time to make phone calls for your project generally believe strongly in what the project is doing. That kind of connection and commitment comes through over the phone and is often contagious.

Phonebanks can be stand-alone fundraising activities or used to follow up a mailing asking for money. When combined with a mailing, the phonebank can be

Adapted from Dennis Quirin, "How to Run a Successful Phonebank," *Grassroots Fundraising Journal,* 2004, 23(4), and materials by Blake Ulveling and other staff at Californians for Justice.

an effective way to have more personal contact, to interact and answer questions, and to remind people to give.

BEST USES

Phonebanks work best when you have a lot of people you want to ask and not enough time to approach each one more personally. However, because of the negative associations with phone solicitations, this strategy also works best when the people you're calling know you or you have some idea that they will be receptive to the cause you're raising money for.

THINGS TO CONSIDER

If you're not able to come up with at least two hundred names to call, you should probably try a different strategy. Volume of calls is what makes phonebanks successful. You also need to find volunteers who are not intimidated by asking for money by phone and who have a cheerful and friendly phone manner.

Note that the national Do Not Call Registry does not apply to nonprofits and charitable organizations. Since October 1, 2003, consumers have been able to register their phone numbers with this federal registry, which prevents businesses from calling to solicit them. Organizations that are exempt from this law include charities or nonprofit organizations, organizations engaged in political solicitations or surveys, and sellers or telemarketers that call *only* consumers with whom they have an established business relationship or from whom they have obtained express written agreement to call. You may want to share this information with your volunteers to reassure them that you can legally call your list. You may, however, still come across an irate person or two who does not want to be called whether they are in the do not call registry or not. Take those people off your list and tell them you are doing so. However, you should confirm whether or not the person still wants to remain on your group's mailing list.

COSTS

You can expect to incur the following costs when doing a phonebank:

- Photocopying
- Refreshments for volunteers (can be donated)

MATERIALS NEEDED FOR VOLUNTEERS

- Tally sheets
- Scripts
- Fact sheets (how to answer common questions)
- Pledge forms
- Call list and tracking form
- Butcher or easel paper for the training and tracking sheets
- Things to make the phonebank fun, such as prizes or noisemakers for people to set off when they get a pledge

STEPS TO TAKE

These are the steps you should plan on taking. Each will be discussed in detail.

1. Make a plan
2. Recruit volunteers
3. Get lists of people to call
4. Find a location for the phonebank
5. Prepare materials
6. Make final preparations
7. Coordinate calling on the night of the phonebank
8. Wrap up

As you go through the steps in detail, use the sample workplan at the end of the chapter to create a timeline and task list.

Step 1: Make a Plan

Decide how much money you want to raise, then figure out how many people you will need to call to reach that goal and how much money to ask for. Here's how to make those calculations:

- One person will average about thirty calls per hour.
- The caller will reach about ten of those people.

- One to three of those people are likely to say yes to making a donation.

- Donations will average $25, though you will often receive gifts of $10 or $15 as well as a few at $100 or more. However, if you know people on the list and have target amounts that you want to ask for, specify that for callers.

Using these rates you can calculate how many people you need to call. If, for example, your goal is to raise $2,500, you would need to call between 1,000 and 1,500 people. With each caller getting through a list of seventy-five names in one evening, you would need between fourteen and twenty people calling. Another option is to have a smaller group of callers making calls over several nights. Aim to have at least five people, which is the number that creates a mood of excitement and a feeling of "We're in this together."

Step 2: Recruit Volunteers

Using the Volunteer Recruitment Form in Resource A, identify people who might be willing to help. If you're part of an established organization, you'll want to ask staff members, board members, volunteers, members, donors, and anyone else who has a positive relationship with the group. While your priority is to find people who are willing to come to the phonebank and make calls, here are some other tasks volunteers can do:

- Find a place to hold the phonebank.

- Help come up with lists of people to call.

- Create the script.

- Help with logistics and arrangements for the day of the phonebank.

Start contacting people you're recruiting to make calls three to four weeks before the phonebank. Make reminder calls the week before the phonebank and again one or two days in advance.

Usually, about half of the people who initially say they'll participate in the phonebank will actually show up. If you need five volunteers to make your phonebank successful, recruit eight to ten volunteers, depending on how committed your volunteers are. It is important that you have a fairly accurate count of who will come because you want to make sure you have enough phone lines for your volunteers. Also, if you've worked hard to get the phone lines available for the calls, it's nice to have volunteers use them.

Step 3: Get Lists of People to Call

Think about who are you calling and why. The size and quality of the list of names you call is probably the single most important factor in how well your phonebank will do. You can have the best phoners, the most delicious food, the nicest office space, and the most compelling reason to be calling—but if you're calling people who don't support your cause, or don't know anything at all about your project, or if you just don't have enough people to call, you will have a difficult time raising the money you need.

A good list contains more than just names and phone numbers. It's best if you have some information about the people you're calling, either from their member or donor records if they are past supporters of the organization or from information you gather from the people who gave you the names. The information can be as basic as who knows them or if and when they've given money before and how much, or as detailed as how they got involved with your organization. Any information you can pass on to the phoners will be helpful for their calls. A good list will also have a space for notes. Part of the benefit of a phonebank is to be able to update information you have about the people in your database. New or wrong numbers are important to note, along with any relevant information you might learn during a call. It's also important to be able to write notes from the call right on the list, such as "No answer," "Left message," or "Call back Tuesday." These notes will inform the next person who calls whether or not you had some contact with the person.

A phonebank is different from many of the other strategies in this book in that you need to have larger lists of people to ask. If each caller can get through a list of seventy-five names in one evening and you're aiming to recruit at least five callers, you'll need at least 375 names to call in order to create the energy, momentum, and ultimate success in meeting your goals.

If your organization already has a mailing list of people the group has come in contact with, that's a good place to start. If you have sign-in sheets from events that you've had, they are a great list to call. (If you do not have sign-in sheets, consider making them a regular part of all your events so that you can build your list of contacts for future fundraising.) You can also use the worksheet in Resource B, "Who Can You Ask," to gather up names and phone numbers of people your phonebank volunteers know. And you might even consider trading lists with organizations that work on issues similar to yours.

Step 4: Find a Location for the Phonebank

Once you've identified who is making the calls and whom you're calling, you need to have phones for people to make the calls on and a place to make the calls. The following questions should help lead you to the phones you need:

Do you or any other volunteers work in an office with multiple phone lines? If so, ask people if you can use the phone on their desk. Most phonebanks take place after regular work hours, from 5:00 or 6:00 P.M. to 9:00 P.M., when most people have left the office. Your job is to get commitments for as many phones as you'll need and make sure to remind everyone whose desk you're borrowing on the day before and the day of the phonebank to clear their desk for the phonebanker's use. Remember to find out how many *lines* there are, not how many actual telephones. An office might have ten telephones, but only five lines that people can use to call out at one time.

Is your location in a building with other groups that would let you borrow their phones and phone lines? Many organizations are willing to let a supervised group of people use their phones. Just make sure you ask one or two weeks ahead of time (or however much time you think they will need) and make all the arrangements clear: which desks and which phone lines you can use; how you will reimburse them for the calls, if needed; how to get into the office and lock up; where the restrooms are; and so on. It's easier to coordinate a phonebank if all the callers are in the same office, but it is possible to coordinate phonebanks that are in different offices that are close to each other.

Can you find an organization in your community (not necessarily in your building) that will let you use their phones? If you have a relationship with a real estate office, a union, or other organization with lots of phones, look into borrowing their offices for an evening phonebank and make the same arrangements as above.

Here are some other ways to create more phones:

- Bring in extra phones for phone jacks that are not being used or for fax machine jacks that could be unplugged for the duration of the phonebanking.

- Use the phone part of fax machines that have a phone attached.

- Use cell phones. Ask your volunteers to bring any cell phones they have on the night of the phonebank. Or see if you can borrow some cell phones from supporters. Using cell phones works best if you are making calls on the weekend—

Saturday mid-morning or Sunday early evenings are the best times to reach people on the weekend—because many cell phone services are free of charge for weekend calling. Free minutes on weekday evenings would also work if the free calling time starts early enough. If you have enough cell phones, you could even do a cell phone party at someone's house.

- As a last resort, if your organization can afford it, think about buying pay-per-minute phones. You can pick up a phone and as many minutes as you'll need relatively cheaply, and if you buy a few phones at once you might be able to negotiate a deal. Investigate where in your area you can find prepaid phones. Often you can purchase them from phone dealers such as T-Mobile or Verizon, or at stores such as 7-Eleven relatively cheaply. If you think you might be using them again it's a good investment.

If you just don't have enough phones for all of the people who come, think of other ways to use people's time. Some people could be working on the paperwork tracking how the phonebank is going or on correspondence to people who make a pledge or charge a donation. Have extra people work on those tasks for a while and then rotate them out when another phoner needs a break. Phone shifts during the phonebank can help to create a team atmosphere.

Step 5: Prepare Materials
Create a packet for each phoner that includes the following items:

- Tally sheet
- Summary tally sheet
- Phone script
- Call list
- Pledge forms
- Butcher or easel paper for training and tallying results

Tally Sheets   Prepare two kinds of tally sheets: a master for each person making calls and one that tabulates the totals of all the calls made during the phonebank.

An individual's tally sheet, as in Worksheet 6.1, should include the phoner's name, the date, and the total amount of time they spent calling. It's also good to have spaces to record how many calls were made, how many people were actually spoken with, how many said yes or no, and the amounts of money raised.

Worksheet 6.1
Phonebank: Individual Tally Sheet

Volunteer Name: _Carly Washington_   Date: _____ _May 26_ _____

Number of hours of calling (in 15-minute increments): _2 hrs. 15 min._

Results

Attempts: 卅 卅 卅 卅 卅 卅 ||

Contacts: 卅 |

Pledges or donations made: ||

Total amount: $ _65_

No: ||||

"Take me off your list": ||

For each call you make, enter a tally mark for *all* of the relevant categories.

For example: 卅

The summary tally sheet will include the totals from all of the individual tally sheets. The summary tally is important because it lets you monitor how your phonebank is really doing. If at the end of the day your results are drastically different from what you expected, you should try to figure out what's working and what's not. This information should be augmented when you check in with your phoners at the end of the day's calling. Worksheet 6.2 provides a sample summary tally sheet.

Phone Script The best phone script is a simple one. Think of the script as an outline of where you want the conversation to go. Most important, people should try not to read the script to the listener. Let your callers know that it's okay to read catch phrases or succinct points from the script, but once they start to read whole chunks of the script, the person on the other end will tune them out.

The goal is to sound as genuine as possible. Callers should talk to the person on the other end as if talking to a friend. That doesn't mean being too casual. Callers should still sound professional without sounding too nervous. It's also important to remember that the voice on the other end of the phone is a person too. The outline for a phone script in Exhibit 6.1 will give you the basic structure. Script 6.1 is a sample phone script. Use the blank worksheet in the back of the book to create your own script.

The most important thing is to engage the person you're speaking to. You are calling people you want to cultivate as supporters of your issue and as donors. Make the call as personal as you can. Get to know who they are and why they believe in your organization or cause. Be clear and read cues. If a person doesn't want to talk, don't force them to. If a person wants to talk a lot, be clear how much time you want to spend on a call. Its OK to say, "It's been great talking with you, but I should get going so we can reach more people tonight." If you're polite, most people will understand.

After the call, make some notes on the call list about how the call went and what you learned from the person about their involvement and interest in your organization. This will help to continue to build a relationship with them in the future.

If your list is small or you will be doing multiple nights of calls, you may want to consider not leaving messages on answering machines. The phonebank's goal is to have actual live contacts; this way, volunteers can prioritize their time on making contacts. Also, if your list is short and you need to call through it a few times or if you are doing phonebanking over several nights, hanging up on answering machines allows you to keep calling back until you actually reach someone. On your last round through the list, you can leave messages on the answering machines of people you have not reached yet to encourage them to give, especially if these are calls to follow up on a mailing.

Worksheet 6.2
Phonebank: Consolidated Tracking Sheet

Number of Volunteers: __7__   Date: __3/12 and 3/14__

Volunteer name	Volunteer hours	Attempts	Contacts	Donations	Total $ (credit cards)	Total $ (pledges)	Total $	Number of No's
Maria	4	81	12	4	$200	—	$200	8
John	3	67	8	3	$50	$100	$150	5
May	4	83	11	3	$80	$40	$120	6
Carolina	4	75	9	3	$50	$70	$120	5
Hal	4	71	10	3	$100	$200	$300	5
Total	19	377	50	16	$480	$410	$890	29

Exhibit 6.1
Phone Script Outline

Introductions

- Introduce yourself.
- Introduce your group.
- Tell them why you're calling ("I'm calling to talk to you about the Campaign for Better Bike Lanes and to ask for your support.").

Engaging the Prospect

- Ask them if they've heard of the project (or organization or campaign), and if they have, ask what they think about it, or what their involvement has been.
- Say briefly what your relationship with the organization is ("I've been involved with this group for the last two years because I really believe in what they're trying to accomplish.").
- Briefly describe what you're raising money for.
- If they seem open to talking in more depth, you could find out how they may have been involved in the organization recently; let them know what is going on at the organization, any exciting recent developments; and talk to them about current work, such as what projects the organization is doing right now.

The Ask

- Ask for a specific amount of money.
- Wait for an answer. Let them respond.

The Wrap-Up

- Answer any follow-up questions.
- Describe the process for making their donation.
- Thank them for their time and, if appropriate, their donation.

Script 6.1
Sample Phone Script

Structure of what to say	What to say
Introduction	"Hello, may I speak to Janice Berger? Hi, this is May Hong. I'm a volunteer with the Campaign for Better Bike Lanes. You recently signed a petition asking the city to expand the number of streets that have bike lanes. I'm calling you tonight as part of a membership drive and to give you an update about our exciting campaign. Do you have a minute?"
If they say no	"When can I call you back?" (Mark on list when to call back and then do call.)
If they say they're not interested	Say thank you politely and hang up. (Mark "not interested" on list.)
If they say yes, explain why you're calling and engage them	"You recently signed a petition to expand the number of streets with bike lanes. Do you bike? Why do you care about this issue?" (Let them answer.) "Glad to hear you're interested. Did you know that the city recently agreed to our proposal?" (Wait for a response.)
If they don't know about it, continue	"We're very excited by this victory, but"—for those who know about the project, you can add, "as you know—the catch is that the city can only provide half of the funds needed to create these bike lanes. We agreed to raise the other half, which is $6,000. We're calling you now to ask you to help us reach our goal."
Check in to see if they have any questions	"Do you have any questions about the project?" (Either answer any questions, or offer to find out the answers if you don't know.)
Make the ask!	"Sounds like you're with us on the need for more bike lanes. We'd like to ask you to join us by making a contribution. Can you join us with a gift of $50?"
Stop and listen. Pause until they say something. If they say yes, they'd like to give	"Thank you so much! If you can pay with a credit card, that's easiest for us. But if you prefer to send in a check, I'll send you a reminder and a return envelope."
If they say no	"Thank you for taking the time to talk to me. Can we call you at another time?" (If they give you the impression that they just can't afford to give right now, and you will be doing another fundraising campaign in the future, it's a good idea to ask if you can contact them again. If they really aren't interested in your project, just thank them and say goodbye.)

Call List   Each caller should receive a list of names with contact information and any other information you have, such as giving history (if applicable), relationship to your group, who knows them, and how you met them or got their name. Also make sure there's space on the form for notes. New or wrong numbers are important to note, along with any relevant information you might learn during a call. It's helpful to have good lists—accurate names, phone numbers, and so on—so that your volunteers do not get too frustrated. However, there will inevitably be a certain percentage of wrong numbers; just make sure your volunteers understand this and know that any new information they learn helps clean up the lists. This is an important job if you want to use these lists again. You also want callers to indicate if they left a message or were told to call back at another time.

It's better to have more names and numbers on your list than you think callers can get through so that your volunteers don't run out of numbers to call. Worksheet 6.3 shows what such a call list should look like.

Pledge Forms   Each volunteer will send out a pledge form like the one in Exhibit 6.2 to people who say they'd like to make a donation. The volunteer should ask if they'd like to pay by check or credit card (if you have the capacity to accept payments by credit card) and be sure to check their correct mailing address. They may have recently moved, or may want to receive the pledge form at a different address than the one on your call list. At the end of the evening, you will photocopy all of the pledge forms and then mail one copy to the donor. Make sure to include a separate thank-you note with the pledge form.

Step 6: Final Preparations

Once you do these few last things before the phonebank night, you're ready to phone.

- Make reminder calls to your volunteers. Emphasize the importance of the phonebank and let them know that there will be a training and snacks. Thank them for agreeing to come.

- Secure as many phones as you'll need on the nights you'll need them.

- Buy, order, or get donations of food or snacks for the night.

- Create any motivational items, like a group "thermometer," to measure the success of the night.

- Figure out any other logistics, such as rides or child care for phoners.

Worksheet 6.3
Sample Call List

This is a list of names you have collected from your own database, from contacts of your volunteers, or from lists of organizations that are willing to share their names with you. This is the list from which your phonebankers will make their calls and record their results.

Name and address	Phone number	History and notes	Result of call	Pledge form sent (and date)	Money collected
Joe Smith 4323 State St. Missoula, MT	(505) 876-1234	Gave $25 in 2003	1st attempt: 9/22, l.m. 2nd attempt: 9/28, spoke to daughter, l.m. with her 3rd attempt: Spoke to Joe, just lost his job, can't give right now		
Roy Sung Address City, State, ZIP	(413) 444-4444	Has given $50/year for past 3 yrs.	1st attempt: 9/22, asked if we could call back later 2nd attempt: 9/24, will give $75!	9/24, sent form	10/5, rcvd. check

```
┌────────────────────────────────────────────────────────────┐
│                        Exhibit 6.2                           │
│                    Sample Pledge Form                        │
├────────────────────────────────────────────────────────────┤
│                                                              │
│  Thank you for your pledge to support our public schools!    │
│  Please mail this form with your payment to the address      │
│  below.                                                      │
│                                                              │
│  Pledge Amount: $_____  Date:_____         │
│                                                              │
│  Name _____                │
│                                                              │
│  Address_____                 │
│                                                              │
│  City, State, ZIP_____  Phone_____   │
│                                                              │
│  E-Mail _____                          │
│                                                              │
│  Payment Option:                                             │
│                                                              │
│  ___ Check (make payable to "Silver City Public School       │
│      Foundation")                                            │
│                                                              │
│  ___ Credit Card (please fill out the following):            │
│                                                              │
│      Card Number _____                     │
│                                                              │
│      Expiration Date_____                     │
│                                                              │
│      Signature_____ Date Signed_____      │
│                                                              │
│  Mail form to Silver City Public School Foundation, P.O.     │
│  Box 5678, Silver City, NM 80000.                            │
│                                                              │
└────────────────────────────────────────────────────────────┘
```

Step 7: The Night of the Phonebank

Your volunteers may be a little nervous at the beginning of the evening. The training you do before the phoning begins can help give them concrete tips and confidence to be successful. Remind them that people are often much more receptive to volunteers and that they should just speak from their heart.

Do a short training at the beginning of the phonebank (about twenty minutes) that includes the following items:

- An icebreaker so that volunteers feel comfortable with each other (something quick, like going around the room saying your name and your favorite food)

- A description of who you are calling and why, as well as a goal for how much money you want to raise that evening (make this goal exciting but doable)

- Review of materials, including the list of people they'll be calling, tally sheet, background on what you're raising money for, and the phone tips in Handout 6.1

- Instructions on how to fill out the paperwork

- Review of the script, frequently asked questions, and difficult questions

- Role plays: Have people pair off and spend five or ten minutes each playing the caller. This is important, even for people who have participated in phonebanks before. Practice will help everyone get more familiar with the process of calling and with the issues they'll be talking about with prospects.

Be sure to take good care of your volunteers during the phonebank.

Provide food. Food doesn't have to be elaborate, but some snacks and drinks will give the volunteers a sense of being taken care of. If some volunteers will be coming right from work, consider providing food that they can eat during the orientation.

Make it fun. Think of ways to create momentum and make the evening enjoyable for your volunteers. For example, when someone gets a yes, celebrate it—fill up a progress thermometer. Give an award to the person who got the rudest no, the most yeses, and so on.

Briefly check in with people every half-hour or so. Ask how it's going, provide pep talks, help solve problems about scenarios that arose, and keep up people's momentum. Check-ins can be as brief as asking, "Is everything going all right?" so you don't get people out of their rhythm.

Provide some closure at the end of the evening. Here are some ways to do that:

- Have people go around and say how it went for them, or check in with people before they leave to find out what their experience was like.

- Give people a chance to briefly share stories about particularly compelling or rude calls.

- Make everyone feel like the night was a big success.

- If you met the evening's goal—celebrate it!

- If you didn't meet the goal, find something positive to highlight in addition to lessons learned for the future.

- If there will be future nights of phonebanking, have people sign up for more shifts or other organizational activities.

Handout 6.1
Phone Tips for Phonebankers

- Be friendly and enthusiastic. Smile! You can tell when someone is smiling even over the phone.

- Assume the listener's support, be confident, and convey urgency.

- Be direct ("We're working to win . . . ," not "We hope to get . . .").

- Adapt the script into your own words—work on sounding conversational.

- Listen; draw people out with open-ended questions to find out why they're interested in your issue.

- If someone asks you a question that you don't know the answer to, be honest and tell them you don't know. If it's an important question, let them know you'll get back to them (and then make a note of it and *do* get back to them yourself or make sure someone else does).

- Keep it short and simple. Be clear, concise, and direct. Tell them why you're calling at the beginning.

- Ask for a specific commitment, a specific amount of money.

- Once you make the ask, be silent (let them think about it and answer; don't fill the space with nervous chatter).

- Close the deal—once they make a specific commitment, thank them and secure the method of payment (check, credit card). If they need to think about it, ask if there are any questions you can answer right now. If they still need to think, get a specific time to call them back (and then follow up).

- Thank them for their time.

- Remember that practice makes perfect!

If you have the capacity to do so and if you are calling a geographic area that makes this feasible, you might consider having someone actually pick up donations throughout the night as people make pledges. While this is labor intensive and requires a volunteer with a car and good people skills, it can be a great way to increase your personal contact with your supporters, and there is a higher chance of actually receiving the check. This especially works if you are calling people in a specific neighborhood or small town. The in-person contact also allows you to do other quick action steps, such as bring the person a yard sign to support your issue, get them to sign a postcard or petition, or collect other forms of donations, such as food and clothing. Some groups have used this tactic very successfully to augment the effectiveness of their phonebanks.

Step 8: After the Phonebank

Once the phonebanking is completed, wrap up this activity with the following tasks:

- Make copies of all pledge forms.
- Mail a copy of each pledge form to the donor with a short note and a reply envelope.
- Make follow-up calls two weeks later to those who haven't fulfilled their pledge.
- Send thank-you notes to volunteers within a week of the phonebanking thanking them for their time and giving them a brief report on the results of the evening.

FIRST-TIME PHONEBANK AT LORETTO ACADEMY

The Loretto Academy, a K–12 Catholic school in El Paso, Texas, ran an incredibly successful first-time phonebank. They were in the midst of a capital campaign to raise funds for some much-needed renovation of their buildings, and they needed to reenergize their campaign efforts and get their board of trustees involved. Since they had never done phonebanking before, the president of the Academy provided an article on phonebanking from the *Grassroots Fundraising Journal* to the development director.

Following the instructions in the article, the development director made a list of students' families who had not contributed to the capital campaign and selected only those who they thought could give a substantial gift. Then she sent the list to their board, asking board members to select families they thought would be responsive to their calls. She printed out lists that contained some biographical information about each family, including the ages of their children and the family's past giving history.

The Academy ran the phonebank on one evening from 6:00 P.M. to 8:00 P.M. Six board members phoned from the phonebank site and five more called from their homes. Board members got the names of the people they had preselected along with others whom no one knew personally. Each volunteer had five to seven families to contact, and they were asked to follow up another time with folks they didn't reach that night.

On the evening of the phonebank, those who called from the school ate sandwiches, reviewed their scripts and the sheet of frequently asked questions, then got on the phones. They were amazed and thrilled when they raised $29,500 from pledges that evening and during follow-up.

While the Loretto Academy is not a small, grassroots organization or project, their annual goal for income from individual donors is only $140,000. The money raised from one evening of phonebanking made up a significant part of that goal. The lesson learned here is that if you have a community of supporters, people interested in your work, and a group of volunteers who are willing to learn, you can run a very successful phonebank.

Thanks to Alejandrina Morton of the Loretto Academy for sharing their experience.

WORKPLAN

The following workplan provides a summary of the key steps necessary to implement this fundraising strategy and an estimated time frame for each step. It is meant to be a template from which to create your own plan and your own timeline. By taking the time to create a plan and timeline, you'll be more organized, more likely to avoid last-minute crises, and ultimately more successful in raising the money you need.

Workplan 6.1
Phonebanks

What	Who	When (Week Number)								Done
		1	2	3	4	5	6	7	8	
1. Make a plan										
Make a budget		x								
Identify potential volunteer roles		x								
2. Recruit volunteers		x	x							
3. Compile lists of people to call			x	x						
4. Find a location			x							
Finalize site and date				x						
5. Prepare materials					x	x				
6. Make final preparations										
Make sure you have enough phone lines					x					

What	Who	When (Week Number)								Done
		1	2	3	4	5	6	7	8	
Arrange for refreshments						x				
Make reminder calls to volunteers					x	x				
7. Hold the phonebank							x			
Follow up on pledges made							x	x		
8. Wrap up									x	

Door-to-Door Fundraising

With door-to-door fundraising, a team of people go from house to house (or apartment to apartment) in a neighborhood to let residents know about a problem facing the people in the community and to suggest an action they can do to help solve the problem, such as signing a petition or writing a letter to a legislator. The fundraiser then ties the subject's interest in the issue to a strong pitch for a contribution.

Door-to-door fundraising, also called canvassing, is one of the more sophisticated fundraising methods in this book. This strategy requires volunteers who are willing to speak to strangers at their door and to ask them for money, and a coordinator to prepare and train the volunteers to feel comfortable in this endeavor. The logistics of preparing materials and running a canvass also require attention to detail. However, if you have an action that you want people to take beyond making a contribution, if you want to identify support within a specific neighborhood, and if you have willing and enthusiastic volunteers, then door-to-door fundraising is a fantastic strategy for you.

Usually, a door-to-door canvass that is primarily a fundraising activity uses paid professional canvassers, and the canvass is an ongoing organizing and fundraising strategy for an established group. It takes a fair amount of training and infrastructure to run a full-scale canvass. However, this strategy can be modified to be used on a much smaller scale as a one-time or periodic event, and it can still be used to identify support for an issue and raise a solid amount of money. In this chapter, we discuss the considerations in deciding whether to embark on a volunteer door-to-door fundraising canvass, how to run an effective canvass, and other activities and follow-up that will help make the canvass worthwhile in the longer term.

BEST USES

There are several reasons to do door-to-door fundraising.

To do education and outreach. Door-to-door fundraising is a great way to share information about an issue one-on-one and to identify supporters. With face-to-face interaction at someone's doorstep, you can smile and look someone in the eye, convey the problems and issues you are working on with passion, and hear and connect with the interests of the person you are speaking to.

To generate action. Canvassing is a great way to generate action, such as signing a petition or postcard, writing a letter to a decision maker, or making a commitment to attend a meeting or event. By getting people to take action, your project can advance its program goals as well as tie the person in as more than someone who only gives money.

To target a geographic area or constituency. By choosing which neighborhoods to canvass, you can target specific constituents geographically or demographically.

To use as a strategy over time. Door-to-door fundraising is a strategy that is best used over time and as part of a larger fundraising and action strategy. While canvassing can be used as a one-time strategy, it is not the fastest, easiest way to generate money in the short term. Volunteers who canvass more than once or twice will begin to strengthen their outreach and fundraising skills and will get better results.

THINGS TO CONSIDER

A canvass can be an extremely effective strategy and a rewarding experience. Its effectiveness depends in large part on the conditions you have in place.

Door-to-door contact work can be daunting for many volunteers, especially when it involves asking strangers for money. That is why it is very important for a coordinator to prepare an upbeat training with plenty of opportunity to role-play so that volunteers can practice what they'll say, get a chance to ask their "what ifs," and to learn the skills in a positive, constructive environment. Confidence and training are *the* most important determinants of success.

The following are a set of questions your group can ask to decide whether a fundraising canvass is the right strategy for you. The more questions you are able to answer positively, the better the chances a canvass will work well for you. Don't worry if you can't answer yes to all these questions. This is just a quick way to get a clearer understanding of what you are working with.

- Do you have a cause that most people in your geographic area will easily relate to, or that can easily be explained at the door?

- Do you have an action step that you want people to take in addition to giving money—such as sign a petition, sign a postcard, or come to a meeting?

- Do you have some volunteers with some experience or enthusiasm to do door-to-door outreach?

- Do you have some volunteers with some experience or enthusiasm to do fundraising?

- Do you know anyone with experience in canvassing or running a fundraising canvass who can help coordinate, train, or give you advice?

- Do you have someone in mind (it may be yourself!) who might be willing to coordinate or learn how to coordinate the canvass?

COSTS

In a traditional door-to-door fundraising canvass with paid staff, the biggest cost is labor. For an all-volunteer effort, the costs are relatively minimal.

- Refreshments for volunteers
- Clipboards and pens
- Flipchart and markers for training
- Carfare

STEPS TO TAKE

These are the steps you should plan on taking. Each will be discussed in detail.

1. Make a plan
2. Recruit volunteers
3. Secure logistics
4. Prepare materials
5. Prepare training for volunteers
6. Go out into the field
7. Evaluate, do paperwork and follow-up

As you go through the steps in detail, use the sample workplan at the end of the chapter to create a timeline and task list.

Step 1: Make a Plan

As emphasized above, it takes time and work to set up a door-to-door canvass, but if you have a compelling neighborhood issue, enthusiastic volunteers, and a willing coordinator, door-to-door fundraising can be extremely effective and rewarding. It is helpful, though not required, to have a coordinator who has had some experience going door-to-door and can provide some training and encouragement to the volunteers. Professional canvass coordinators will tell you that the key to a successful canvass is training, training, training. If the coordinators do not have door-to-door experience, we recommend that the coordinators do a trial run of the canvass to test out the materials, get a feel for what to say, and build the confidence to train and support others. Conveying confidence and enthusiasm will go a long way with your volunteers.

Expected Income   To figure out how much money your fundraising canvass can make, use the following equation:

$$\text{Number of contributions per hour} \times \text{average contribution} \times \\ \text{hours on doors} \times \text{number of volunteers} = \text{total dollars}$$

Results will vary depending on how receptive the neighborhood is, how well volunteers are trained, and so on. However, you can use the following numbers as a rough guide: A volunteer will generally be able to talk to about ten people (many people are not home, busy, or do not want to speak with you) during two full hours of going door to door. Of that number, one or two will give money. Those people will give varying amounts, but the average gift will probably be about $25, so each volunteer will bring in a total of $25 to $50. With ten volunteers, then, the team could raise between $250 and $500 in one two-hour shift.

Keep in mind that many all-volunteer fundraising canvasses have raised much more money than this because the cause was very close to the hearts of the neighbors or the average gift was higher. Given the variation in communities, this equation presents a fairly conservative, and therefore realistic, goal to set. In some communities, more people are home on a Saturday afternoon or a weekday evening than we have calculated here. In some rural areas, there may be more distance between houses, making it harder to reach as many people in a couple of hours; in some smaller communities, however, the neighbors are friendly, making it is easier to raise money there. In larger cities, housing is more dense, allowing canvassers to go to many more doors, but some people have become suspicious of people coming to their door and will simply wave you away or won't want to talk to you.

Who and Where to Canvass   Since going door-to-door is an ideal way to reach a geographic area or a geographically organized constituency, who you decide to try to reach depends on your project's mission or approach. Here are some potential ways to approach your canvass. Keep in mind that people most directly affected by your issue are your prime audience.

- If you are trying to raise money for the local school arts program, families with children at the school are likely to be supportive.

- If you are trying to mobilize African-American renters to testify for eviction-protection legislation at city hall, try canvassing apartments in predominantly African-American neighborhoods.

- If you are canvassing to retain low-income health programs such as Medicaid, low-income neighborhoods would have a high number of people with a direct interest in your issue.

For all of these causes, however, there will also be people who may not be so directly affected but who are sympathetic. More liberal, middle-class parts of town may have people who are not direct beneficiaries of the need but who may have shared values and would be willing to make a contribution and take action as well. Do not assume, however, that higher-income people will necessarily give more money than lower-income people. In fact, a professional canvasser working on low-income health-care issues reported that some of her best fundraising nights were in low-income neighborhoods, where people most affected by the issues gave more money to the canvass. If the issue is close to people's hearts, you make a compelling case, and you ask, people will give.

The Benefits of Repetition   You can certainly plan to do a one-time canvass. However, because people's skills improve over time, if you have willing volunteers you might consider doing canvassing at least during a couple of weekends. The materials and training will already be prepared and the learning curve for everyone involved will help make your canvass more effective as people practice and build their confidence.

The Flow of the Day   Depending on what you think will work better for your volunteers, you might want a weekend day's door-to-door canvass schedule to look something like this:

10:00–11:15	Training
11:15–11:30	Grab snacks and go to the field
11:30–1:30	Canvass
1:30–2:00	Return, do paperwork, debrief, sign up for future activities

If your volunteers have the energy, they could stay out and go door-to-door for three hours, but more than that might be too exhausting. If you want people to stay out in the field longer, send them out with a lunch and snacks. Another variation, if you think your volunteers would be willing, is to have a more thorough, two-hour training on a separate evening and then sign people up for specific canvass shifts on different days. However, experience shows that you can probably make more effective use of time and make sure that everyone gets the training if the training and canvass are on the same day.

Use Worksheet 7.1, Door-to-Door Fundraising Planning, to help you think about what you need to consider in planning your canvass.

Step 2: Recruit Volunteers

Volunteers are the heart of a fundraising canvass. The number of volunteers you will need depends on your fundraising goals, but the more canvassers, the better your chances will be to raise money. The synergy that comes from having more people can help boost people's spirits and increase their effectiveness. Volunteers who have some outreach or fundraising experience are ideal, but enthusiasm (or at least willingness to learn) is good enough. Ideally, you would have at least ten volunteers show up, which means that you should get fifteen to twenty people to commit. Usually, about half to two-thirds of the people you have signed up to do something will

Door-to-Door Fundraising Planning

What is the problem you are working to address?

Public funding of schools in our state has been slashed in half over the last 3 years. As a result, our local school, Lincoln Elementary, is proposing to cut its art programs, after-school mentoring programs, and special education programs.

What is the solution you propose?

Parents and kids want schools, not jails! We demand that the state budget for education be increased 5 percent, and the budget for incarcerating our young people be decreased 10 percent.

What specific action steps are you asking people to take?

Come join our group, Lincoln Parents for Schools Not Jails, for three important actions: (1) Speak out at the local school board on June 2nd. (2) Get on the bus and join hundreds of parents September 1st at the state capitol to send a message to the governor. This is just before school starts, so bring your kids! (3) Give money to pay for bus to state capitol.

Who is most affected by your issue? Who else cares about this issue? How would you reach these groups? What neighborhoods do these groups live in?

- *Lincoln Elementary School parents, especially parents with kids enrolled in programs threatened with cuts—art programs, after-school mentoring, and special education. Try to get list of students and parents in those programs; petition and recruit at Open House.*
- *PTA Parent Action Committee—meet one on one with key committee members at their homes.*
- *Parents and neighbors near the school—go door-to-door in 10 blocks surrounding school.*

Do you have volunteers with some experience asking for money or doing outreach to help coordinate and to canvass? Who are the other volunteers you would like to recruit?

Alejandra and Tom—are very active with the PTA Parent Action Committee. They have done petitioning outside the school and local grocery stores about a lot of issues.

Karen, Helen, and Daren helped with the playground fundraising drive two years ago and have experience asking individuals for small to large sums of money up to $500.

Ed, Maria, Sara, Michael, Laura, and Bonnie—are enthusiastic parents. Recruit them!

What contribution levels will you ask for? What will be the payment method? What is your projected fundraising goal.

Fundraising goal: $2000

Costs: $25—brown-bag lunch for a family, $50—an hour of translation, $150-rent sound equipment, $500 will sponsor a bus!

In-kind photocopying and food for volunteers.

Pitch: Support the Parent Caravan to the state capitol! Pay by check.

What follow-up do you have the capacity to do?

Alejandra, Ed, and Bonnie will make follow-up calls: make sure people send in pledges.

In the summer, in August—call donors to thank them and invite them to join the caravan.

show up. For a task that is a bit more daunting, like a canvass, you might get more people who beg out at the last minute, so err on the side of recruiting more people.

Encourage all your prospective volunteers with the message that even if they have never done door-to-door fundraising before, you will provide training and support to help them succeed. Volunteers who end up participating will be particularly valuable to your project because their level of commitment is high and the outreach and fundraising skills that they develop can translate in valuable ways to other work your project takes on.

Be sure to call volunteers a week before your canvassing session and then again the night before to remind them where and when to meet, give them directions on how to get there, go over the entire time commitment, and suggest that they wear comfortable shoes. Reaffirm how important this canvassing is, that there will be a fun training, and that your group is counting on them to be there.

The door-to-door fundraising experience will be much more positive and effective if volunteers can support and encourage each other. If possible, examine the list of volunteers who commit to coming to identify volunteers who have experience or who can take some leadership. You might even want to tell them ahead of time that you would like them to play a supportive role—that way they will come expecting to help out and will probably take their commitment more seriously and be more likely to come. On the day of the canvass, once volunteers have arrived, have someone who is not helping with the training take a moment to make teams in which, as much as possible, newer people are paired with more experienced people.

Step 3: Secure Logistics

The logistics of door-to-door fundraising can be complicated, so being organized can make a big difference in how successful your volunteers are and how happy they are with their experience. Identify space where volunteers can be trained, launched into the field, and return to after the canvass to debrief and do paperwork. This can be someone's home, a church hall, or a school cafeteria. Ideally, the send-off site would be within walking distance of where people will be canvassing. Make any needed arrangements for transportation if the site is not close to the canvass area or if the area to be canvassed is very large.

Have good maps of the neighborhood so it will be easy to show volunteers which streets they are to canvass. Be clear about which team covers which streets and areas so there is no overlap—mark the maps carefully with the boundaries of the area they are to go door-to-door in.

Step 4: Prepare Training for Volunteers

The success of door-to-door fundraising comes from training and practice. Clarity, confidence, and the organization of the training will transfer to the confidence of your volunteers. The basic concepts and tips that people pick up and the role-playing they do will be important in how effective and confident they are, how strong their interactions will be, and how much money they will be able to raise.

Your training should give enough information so that people have the basics of what they need and have some confidence, but not be so detailed that the main points are lost or that volunteers feel overwhelmed. Sometimes when people are nervous, they think that having more information and being able to answer every possible question that people they canvass might ask will be the magic pill to make that knot in their stomach go away. Instead, keep the training simple, spend a good amount of time having people role-play so they can practice what they will say out loud and get feedback, encourage them with your confidence that they can do it and the understanding that practice makes perfect, and then get them out on the doors.

The following is a sample training that you can adjust for use in your own canvass.

ONE-HOUR CANVASS TRAINING

(10 minutes)	People arrive, sign in, get snacks and coffee.
(5 minutes)	Introductions: Name, where you live, why you're here, your biggest fear about asking for money.
(5 minutes)	Asking for money: Getting over our fears and why it's important to ask. Include the following content:

Question: Who here gives money? Why?

Presentation: As we learned from our introductions, many people are afraid of asking for money. However, from our own experience, we have learned that when we give, we feel that we are contributing to something important, bigger. Many people actually feel touched that someone bothered to knock on their door to chat with them. Remember this as we go out on the doors.

Where money comes from: Using the material in Chapter One, talk about why it's important to raise money from within your community and the fact that 70 percent of Americans donate to causes they believe in.

(10 minutes) *Why we are here today:* Our project's goals, update and education on the issue. Go over materials in the volunteers' packets and explain logistics.

(10 minutes) *Tips for canvassing:* Go over the tips in Handout 7.1, Canvassing Dos and Don'ts, and give volunteers these tips copied from the back of the book. Review Script 7.1, "Sample Conversation at the Door," that follows.

(20 minutes) Lead the following two role-play suggestions, done in pairs. Alternate role-play method: Do a round robin with the entire group or split in two groups. In a round robin, each person, one-by-one, practices speaking to the person next to them in front of the entire group. The person gets feedback from the coordinator and the entire group, and then it is the next person's turn. This method takes more time, but the learning and quality control are much stronger because people see a variety of role-plays and get more feedback.

1. Practice the opening when someone opens the door. Demonstrate once to the large group. Then get people to practice in pairs and give feedback on what they did well and then what could be improved. Ask the trainees to be as specific and concrete as possible with their feedback. Debrief as a group.

2. Practice the ask—asking for a contribution. Demonstrate once in large group. Then get people to practice in pairs and give feedback. Debrief as a group.

Gather materials and get out onto the doors!

Dos

Use positive and strong body language. Smile and use eye contact. At least half your communication comes through body language. Smile even as you're approaching the house—often people peek out the window to see who is coming. Eye contact conveys trust and confidence. (Sometimes there are cultural variations of how much eye contact to have. Adjust to fit what is appropriate for your community.)

Use strong, confident "down tones." Avoid using "up tones" or a questioning tone; instead, use statements. Tone is critical in conveying confidence and makes a big difference in your fundraising. Sometimes in daily conversation, we say statements in questioning tones: "Hi, my name is Maria? I'm with Just Housing? We're a group that's working to increase renter protections? Can I talk to you about this?" Instead, say, "Hi, my name is Maria. I'm with Just Housing. We're working to increase renter protections, and we're fundraising to make that happen. Take a look."

Assume support. Confidence, strong language, and a positive attitude can be contagious. Say, "So I'm sure you're well aware that . . ." instead of "Did you know that . . . ?" Say, "Here, take a look" instead of "Could you look at this?" Even if you just had a less successful interaction, approach each new person with enthusiasm.

Keep it short and simple. The emphasis of this strategy is to keep the interaction to about five or ten minutes. Clearly state the problem your project is addressing and the solution you are working toward, and ask clearly for what you want.

Have materials to hand to the person at the door after your introduction. First, establish eye contact and make your introduction with your materials at your side. Then, if you have a petition on a clipboard, hand the clipboard to the person. It legitimizes what you are saying, and if the person takes the clipboard, it is a sign that they are willing to listen.

Be flexible, mirror the person and use what works. It is important to respond to different people by modifying what you say, increasing the amount you ask for if they are very enthusiastic, still asking for a more modest donation if the person cannot afford the full, initial donation.

Ask for a specific amount, then be silent! Asking for a specific amount helps the person be clear about what you are asking for, and usually you get what you ask for. Our tendency is to fill silence with nervous chatter. Instead, after asking, be quiet and let them answer. Respond only after they have finished.

Respond, give options, then close the deal. You may want to provide payment options—lump sum, split over two or three payments, postdate check. Try to get a check instead of cash since it is safer for you to carry around, and people tend to give more by check. If your project can possibly take credit cards, this will increase the rate of giving.

Remember that no's are part of the equation. Between one-third and one-half of the people we actually talk to during the canvass will make a financial contribution. If you aren't getting no's, that means you're not asking enough people!

Thank people for their time. Whether they give or not, thank them for having listened, and be very sincerely thankful for any size of gift.

Some Don'ts

Don't waste time on people who disagree. Respectfully disagree, thank them, and move on. In the time you spend arguing with someone who disagrees, you could be meeting many people who agree with you who just need to be activated.

Don't bumble. It's natural to be nervous, but don't come across as unprepared and bumbling because you have not practiced what you are going to say and have not familiarized yourself with how to deal with put-offs or how to answer key questions they are likely to raise. Do role-plays and ask questions before going out.

Don't waste time wandering around. Be efficient about your time.

Don't talk too much. You can talk yourself into and right back out of the gift. Let the other person talk. Show interest in the people you meet.

Don't arouse suspicion about who you are and what you are doing. While you don't have to be dressed up, look nice. Walk purposefully and don't loiter. Don't peer in people's windows to see if they are coming, and don't open the door yourself.

Don't talk too much about personal matters or world events. Make a personal connection, but stay focused on your mission.

Don't pretend to understand someone if you don't. Feel free to ask clarifying questions and encourage the person to explain what they mean.

Don't leave without asking for the money.

Use common sense. Don't pat a dog that seems unfriendly, don't cross a freeway, and don't go down a block that you haven't been assigned.

Adapted from "Doorknocking and Fundraising Tips" (Californians for Justice) and "The Five Basic Skills of Field Canvassing" and "Secondary Skills in the Field" (Progressive Action Network).

Step 5: Prepare Logistics and Materials

Good preparation will help your volunteers have a successful day. The following is a list of logistical arrangements and materials that need to be prepared, followed by sample materials that you can adjust and use.

Logistical Arrangements   There are a few things that need to be done ahead of time, including making some arrangements and gathering materials for volunteers to take into the field.

- Arrange for transportation if necessary.
- Prepare two maps for each pair of canvassers. Two people will go down each street—one on one side and one on the other. They should keep track of each other. Clearly mark the maps to show where each pair should go and where they should return at the end of the scheduled time.
- Prepare a master map for the coordinator, particularly if someone is driving the canvassers to a destination and then picking them up.
- Provide an emergency phone contact number for each canvasser to call the coordinator.

Materials for the Field   Each canvasser should have the following materials to take with them into the field:

- ☐ Script for conversation at the door (Script 7.1)
- ☐ A clipboard with a Canvass Tracking Sheet (Worksheet 7.2) taped on the back
- ☐ Project brochures, background information, press clips
- ☐ Blank petition, if using (see Exhibit 7.1)
- ☐ Flyers and fact sheets on the issues
- ☐ Pledge forms (see Exhibit 7.2)
- ☐ Map of the blocks the canvasser is assigned to
- ☐ Pens (at least two in case one is lost or runs out of ink)
- ☐ Medium-size envelopes for collecting checks, credit card slips, and cash
- ☐ Name tag with canvasser's name and the project's name to give the canvasser legitimacy
- ☐ A bottle of water
- ☐ Optional: snacks and lunch

Script 7.1
Sample Conversation at the Door

The basic structure of a conversation at the door that is outlined here can be applied to any issue you want to canvass on. Your volunteers should use this as a guideline, but emphasize to them that they should be conversational and not read from this outline.

Structure of what to say	What to say
Introduction—who you are, the organization you represent, what you are there for, what you want	"Hi, my name is Maria and I'm with People Organized to Win (POW). We're concerned neighbors working on a 'Dump That Dump' campaign to get rid of the toxic waste dump on the corner of Jackson and 11th, and we're fundraising to make that happen. Here, take a look." (Hand clipboard.)
Problem—one- or two-sentence summary of the problem that you are organizing around. In this section, confirm the person's support.	"I'm sure you're well aware that the toxic dump has been there for years. Of course, it's in our neighborhood because they think we're poor, people of color." (Pause and wait for response. May be a nod, or they may say something.)
Solution—one or two sentences to educate the person as to what your organization is doing about it	"That's why we're going to the City Council to demand that they get rid of this dump and test the residents and homes to see what effect it's had on all of us."
Confirmation	"I'm sure you're with me on that." (*Pause and wait for them to respond.*)
Bridge—link the person's agreement with the issue to the need to make a contribution	"Yes, it sounds like you're upset about this dump too. The only way we're going to win is with strong community support and funding. That's why I need you to sign this petition and back that up with a contribution."

Structure of what to say	What to say
The ask—ask for a specific amount, and be straightforward	"Our goal is $60 to get our neighborhood to stand up for our rights and to 'dump that dump'!"
If they say no, provide options, connect the money and the issue, and close the deal. Identify why they are saying no. Respond by acknowledging their issue, reassuring them, connecting the issue and money, and by providing options.	"Is that too much, or is this a bad time?" (If bad time:) "Sure, I totally understand. We have a pledge system, and you can date your check a month in advance if you like." (If too much money:) "Sure, I hear you. The reason we're asking high is because we're up against industries with deep pockets. You can split that payment over two payments—one check now and you can postdate another check." (Or) "We have another level at $48."
If they say yes	"Thanks! Your contribution will make a big difference. You can make your check out to People Organized to Win."
Action piece—it is important to get people to take action besides giving money. Do this *after* asking for money.	"Great, now we'd like to get your signature here on a postcard asking our city council member, Ms. Moneybags, to do the right thing and advocate hard to get rid of that dump. Can you also join us at the city council meeting at 7:00 P.M. next Wednesday?"
Thank them!	"Thank you for your time and contribution, and we'll see you next Wednesday at 7:00 P.M.!"

Worksheet 7.2
Individual Canvass Tracking Sheet

Use this sheet for each canvasser to track their results. If you are using clipboards or folders, you can tape this on the back so that they can easily make "hatchmarks" as they go. The End-of-Canvass Checklist reminds each person what they need to do before leaving.

Name: _Jasmine Lewis_   Phone: _500-667-1230_

Where Canvassed: _1400–1700 blocks of Magnolia St._   Date: _6/23_

Hour	Number of homes visited	Number of contacts	Number of actions	Number of gifts	Amount of cash	Amount of check
1	ℍℍ ℍℍ ℍℍ ℍℍ ℍℍ ℍℍ	ℍℍ ꟷ	ꟷꟷꟷꟷ	ꟷꟷꟷ	$20	$50
2	ℍℍ ℍℍ ℍℍ ℍℍ ℍℍ ꟷꟷ	ꟷꟷꟷ	ꟷꟷ	ꟷ		$35
3	ℍℍ ℍℍ ℍℍ ℍℍ ℍℍ ꟷꟷ	ꟷꟷꟷꟷ	ꟷ	ꟷꟷ	$10	$20
Total		13	7	6	$30	$105

End-of-Canvass Checklist

☐ Filled out individual tracking sheet

☐ Posted results on butcher paper

☐ Turned in all checks, credit cards, and cash

☐ Analyzed results in debrief

☐ Signed thank-you letters for people who gave today

Exhibit 7.1
Sample Petition

Dump That Dump!

The toxic dump on the corner of Jackson and 11th has been in our neighborhood for way too long.

The dump is unsightly, but most important, our children play in the streets, and we do not want them to be exposed to the garbage and toxins. Our community is primarily low-income, working-class people who are mostly people of color. The lack of enforcement of waste disposal laws, the lack of attention to this matter despite complaints from residents, and the dumping in the first place show a pattern of discrimination and racism.

We demand that the City Council:

1. Dump That Dump! Remove the dump from our community!

2. Enforce and strengthen the laws that require these corporations to dispose waste safely. Don't just move it to another neighborhood.

3. Invest $50,000 to test the residents in the area for exposure to toxins.

4. Set up a committee—made up 60 percent of area residents—to oversee the initial test and to explore next steps.

Signature	Name	Address	City and ZIP	Phone	E-mail	Amount	Action	Notes

Canvasser Name: _____ Phone: _____ Date: _____ Location in Field: _____

```
┌─────────────────────────────────────────────────────────────┐
│                        Exhibit 7.2                            │
│                    Sample Pledge Form                         │
│  ───────────────────────────────────────────────────────     │
│                                                               │
│  Yes! I'll join People Organized to Win!                      │
│                                                               │
│  Here's my membership dues of $_____.            │
│                                                               │
│  Name_____            │
│                                                               │
│  Address _____          │
│                                                               │
│  City_____ ZIP _____           │
│                                                               │
│  Phone_____ E-mail_____           │
│                                                               │
│  _____ Yes, I'll come to the city council meeting on          │
│        Wednesday, May 15, at 7:00 P.M.                        │
│                                                               │
│  _____ Yes, I'd like to be part of the "Rapid Response        │
│        Team" to write letters and make phone calls to         │
│        politicians and legislators about the dump             │
│        and other important issues for our community.          │
│                                                               │
│  _____ Yes, I'd like to attend a membership meeting.          │
│                                                               │
└─────────────────────────────────────────────────────────────┘
```

The petition is a useful way to summarize your issue and gives the person something to look at. It can also be used as a way to engage the person you are speaking to. If they take it, it shows that they are interested, and it prompts them to make an initial commitment by taking action and signing. The petition form, shown in Exhibit 7.1, also allows you to get people's names and track where you've been.

Pledge forms like the one in Exhibit 7.2 make the interaction concrete and can reinforce a commitment to attend a meeting or take other action.

At the Training and Debriefing Site Have the following at the site where training and debriefing will occur:

- ☐ Signs for outside to identify the site
- ☐ Volunteer sign-in sheet
- ☐ Refreshments and snacks

- [ ] Paper cups, plates, utensils, napkins
- [ ] Extra pens
- [ ] Butcher or easel paper
- [ ] Markers
- [ ] Masking tape
- [ ] Sample tracking sheet and coordinator's report (Worksheet 7.3) on butcher or easel paper

Step 6: Go Out into the Field

A coordinator should have a cell phone and access to a car in case people need a ride and in case of emergencies. For a small canvass, the coordinator can go out in the field with everyone else and return to the site fifteen minutes early to receive people as they return. For a larger canvass, a coordinator may want to stay at the site to troubleshoot any issues that may come up and to be there in case people show up late or return early.

Step 7: Evaluate, Do Paperwork, and Follow Up

As people return from going door-to-door, they will be tired; have drinks and snacks ready to greet them as they come in. Some canvassers will be frustrated, others will be inspired. The job of the coordinator is to make sure that people feel appreciated, help them debrief and learn from their experience, make sure they give each other constructive feedback, draw out the positive stories, and make sure that people know how to track their results and do the paperwork.

Doing the Paperwork   This is not the most exciting part of the process, but it helps to track your results accurately so that you can evaluate your efforts, and it is crucial that you have good systems to handle the money that you raise. After people catch their breath, ask them to fill out their individual canvass tracking sheets. Then they should put their results up on the Canvass Results Sheet taped to the wall. Have a good system for people to turn in all their membership or donation pledge forms, checks, cash, or credit card forms. Have people write brief, personal thank-you notes to the people who gave and clip each thank-you note to the person's pledge form and money. After the day is over, a couple of

Worksheet 7.3
Canvass Coordinator Report

Copy this sheet onto butcher or easel paper for canvassers to record their results after the canvass. They should transfer their results from the Individual Canvass Tracking Sheet onto the butcher paper. This way, during the debrief, everyone can see the collective results and analyze the day. The coordinator can use this sheet to track the results in case of future canvassing. The end-of-canvass checklist reminds the coordinator what to do before leaving.

Name: _____ Date: _____ Phone: _____ Where canvassed: _____

Name	Hours out	Number of homes visited	Number of contacts	Number of actions	Total number of gifts	Total amount of gifts	Checks	Cash
Sandra Chen	2	25	15	14	2	$20		$20
Carolina Ramirez	2	6	4	4	3	$30	$15	$15
Total	4	31	19	18	5	$50	$15	$35

Evaluation of the Day
Strengths

Challenges

Solutions

End-of-Canvass Checklist

☐ Make sure people fill out their Individual Tracking Sheet.

☐ Collect pledges, checks or cash, and thank-you notes from canvassers.

☐ Double-check that everything is filled out and that the money matches the pledges.

☐ Double-check thank-you letters and send them out.

☐ Deposit checks.

☐ Make sure there is a follow-up plan for all action items.

coordinators should go through all the paperwork to make sure that everything is filled out correctly, that the thank-yous are addressed and mailed, that the donations get processed, and that all the needed follow-up is highlighted and planned for.

Here is an example of a thank-you note canvassers can write.

> Dear LaRaye,
>
> It was great to meet you at your house today. Thanks for your contribution to the No Big Box in Our Town Campaign. Your $35 membership means a lot to us and will help us sustain our work.
>
> Just a reminder that the public meeting with Big Box's regional manager, Ray Cist, and City Council member Don Nothing will be on Tuesday, July 25, at 11:00 A.M., and we're very excited that you'll be there. We have you signed up to tell how you used to work for Big Box in a nearby town and that you got paid minimum wage and no health benefits, and that they have a pattern of treating all the black workers badly. Your story will be strong testimony.
>
> Again, we're excited you're joining our campaign and we'll see you soon!
> Sincerely,
> Maria Martinez

Debrief, Evaluate, and Accentuate the Positive   Strong evaluation and debriefing sessions after the canvass are especially valuable for helping people analyze and learn from their challenges, celebrate their successes, and feel enthusiastic to do more.

The most rewarding part of door-to-door fundraising is when people get to share stories about all the great people they met. Start your debrief with this to set a positive tone. Without fail, canvassers will speak about being inspired by someone who is affected by the issue or about feeling appreciative that someone simply thanked them for being out talking to people. Encourage people to share these stories and what worked for them.

People will also need to commiserate about the inevitable doors slammed, dogs that chased them, and turndowns they got. If people had a challenging time, troubleshoot together to think about specific solutions to problems that arose.

If people felt enthusiastic, try to schedule one or two more door-to-door fundraising sessions. Everyone's work will improve significantly every time they go out in the field, especially if people get useful, specific feedback and have a positive experience.

Plan Follow-Up Activities   At the end of your canvassing sessions, document all your materials used, results, and contacts. The contacts that you've made can build your project in other ways. Identify any people to follow up with: those who were enthusiastic about your issue or want to volunteer or play some role. Of course, everyone who gave should be tracked so that they can be asked to give again.

Your volunteers are now stars and have honed a set of skills that will be invaluable for your project. Thank your volunteers for their hard work and find future leadership opportunities for them.

VARIATIONS ON THE THEME

Doing "personal visits" with a specific group of people. If you belong to a school, church, union, or other institution, you can get a list of members or potential supporters and make personal visits to speak with them about the issue, identify their support, and ask them for a contribution. Some Christians may be familiar with the yearly "all-church canvass," where members of the church stewardship committee visit all active church members to ask them to make their yearly pledge. If you are working to keep your daughter's elementary school arts programs funded, for example, members of the school's Parent Teacher Association or a list of parents of the after-school arts program are great audiences to approach for support. Do your best with whatever list you can find or develop. You could split the list by geography and knock on people's doors just as outlined in this chapter.

Canvassing people at a busy public place or at businesses frequented by people receptive to your issue. With a canvass of this nature, where the canvasser stands at a busy corner or outside a business, interactions are shorter, people are more in a hurry and tend to give smaller amounts, but you can make many more contacts and identify more supporters in a short amount of time.

In addition to the tips in this chapter, here are a few more that are specific for this type of outreach:

- Use strong body language to engage people in conversation. Walk alongside them, slightly in front but facing them so that they can see you and stop to look at your clipboard and materials if they wish.

- Don't stand behind a table and hope people will come up to you. If you have a table or an ironing board with materials, stand in front of it and move so that you can approach people.

- Keep it short and simple. Brevity is an even more important skill here because people are on their way into a store or to their car. You have about a three-second window to catch their attention enough to stop them.

- Have people sign a petition. While they sign their name and give their contact information, build and document support for your issue. If they agree to volunteer, to donate, or if they want more information, you already have their contact information.

- Ask them for a donation of $1 to $20. Because the interaction is shorter and in a public place, the person will probably give less than if they were at their home.

WORKPLAN

The following workplan provides a summary of the key steps necessary to implement this fundraising strategy and an estimated time frame for each step. It is meant to be a template from which to create your own plan and your own timeline. By taking the time to create a plan and timeline, you'll be more organized, more likely to avoid last-minute crises, and ultimately more successful in raising the money you need.

Workplan 7.1
Door-to-Door Fundraising

What	Who	1	2	3	4	5	6	7	8	Done
1. Make a plan										
Identify coordinators		x								
Set fundraising and volunteer turnout goals		x								
Decide who and where to contact and how to talk about issue		x								
Picture the flow of the day		x								
Identify potential volunteer roles			x							
2. Recruit volunteers										
Make calls to recruit volunteers			x	x						
3. Secure logistics										
Identify space to do send-off and debrief			x							
Make transportation plan if needed			x	x						
4. Prepare materials										
Adjust the script to fit your issue				x	x					
Copy tracking sheets, informational flyers, and other needed papers				x	x					
Prepare all other materials needed for the day				x	x					

What	Who	When (Week Number)								Done
		1	2	3	4	5	6	7	8	
5. Prepare training for volunteers										
Recruit trainers			x	x						
Adjust training to fit your issue				x	x					
Do a test run of the canvass with coordinators and trainers						x				
6. Go out in the field										
Do training with volunteers on the day (or before, if needed)							x			
Go out in the field							x			
7. Evaluate, do paperwork, and follow up										
Debrief, evaluate, and celebrate with the volunteer team										
If possible, schedule one to three more canvassing sessions						x	x	x		
Do paperwork, document the event						x	x	x	x	
Send out thank-yous						x	x	x	x	

Social Gatherings

House Parties

A great way to raise money is the tried-and-true house party. With this strategy, someone invites friends and acquaintances to a gathering at their house to learn more about the work of an organization or campaign. At the house party they are asked to make a contribution. In the weeks before the party, the host sends out invitations, makes calls to make sure friends are coming, and asks them to make a contribution if they can't attend. At the party itself, guests socialize and eat good food and drink. Midway through the party, the host and members of the organization hold a short program to educate and engage the guests on the project and the issues and then make a "pitch" to ask people to make a contribution. Guests happily do so and then continue munching on food and drink.

House parties can raise several hundred to several thousand dollars. With an invitation list of at least eighty people, you can expect to raise $1,000 if you carefully follow the steps in this chapter.

BEST USES

The comfortable atmosphere of holding the house party at someone's home and the fact that guests have some relationship with the host make for a friendly setting in which they can get to know the project and give money. It's good to hold a house party when you have the following ingredients:

- An enthusiastic person who is willing to tap into their networks, make the calls, and work to make sure people come to the party

- A need to raise money quickly

- A desire to introduce new people to a project and to get them to contribute for the first time

- A house that people would enjoy coming to because of its comfort, location, and the like

THINGS TO CONSIDER

Of all the fundraising strategies described in this book, house parties are among the easiest to organize. They can be carried out by one or two people, completed in a brief period of time (about one month from planning to execution), and don't cost much money to do. The key consideration in choosing a house party over something else is whether you have a large enough list of people to invite who either care a lot about the cause or like the host enough to come even if they don't know the cause or their belief in it isn't particularly strong.

To calculate how much money you'll raise, assume that the average contribution will be between $20 and $50 and that some people will send you money even if they can't attend. Plan that between 25 and 35 percent of the people you invite will attend the party.

COSTS

- Postage for invitations.

- Copying costs for the invitation, reply card, and informational materials about the project

- Envelopes for mailing and reply

- Food and drink

STEPS TO TAKE

These are the steps you should plan on taking. Each will be discussed in detail.

1. Find the host and make a plan

2. Prepare an invitation list

3. Prepare and send the invitations

4. Make follow-up calls

5. Prepare the agenda, practice the pitch, and hold the party

6. Send thank-yous

7. Evaluate the event

As you go through the steps in detail, use the sample workplan at the end of the chapter to create a timeline and task list.

Step 1: Find the Host and Make a Plan

Find a host. Finding a host is the very first step in planning the party. An enthusiastic person who is willing to follow the steps outlined in this chapter is key to the house party's success. If there is more than one house party host for your project and you are planning a series of parties, you may want to have all the hosts gather at the beginning to make sure they are clear about what steps are needed to make a successful house party and what the timeline is.

House parties usually take four to six weeks to organize, but they can be organized in as little time as two weeks. It takes between sixteen and twenty hours of work to make a successful house party. Here is how the time is generally spent:

Two hours to prepare the invitation list and get all the addresses

Two to four hours to write the invitation, buy the invitation materials, and make copies

Two hours to do the mailing

Four hours to make follow-up calls

Four to six hours to prepare for and host the house party

One hour to write notes

One hour to evaluate

Choose a house for the party. Although most people host a house party at their own home, you may find that someone is an ideal host because they have a wide circle of friends they're willing to invite, but doesn't have a large enough house to accommodate them. Consider finding another volunteer to lend their home to the event. Having more than one host is also an option if you want to increase the number of people you can invite.

Choose a date and time. House parties are usually scheduled to go on for two hours; best times are weekend afternoons, although weekday evenings can also work.

Step 2: Prepare an Invitation List

We suggest that you invite four times the number of people you want at the party. About a third of the people invited will say that they can come, but in the end only about one-fourth will actually get there. Along with thorough follow-up calls, inviting one hundred people should bring about twenty-five people to a house party; inviting forty people should bring about ten. Tap into your networks! Brainstorm as large a guest list as the group and the host can based on how many people the house can accommodate. For ideas on who to invite, see Resource B, Who Can You Ask?

Tracking down people's addresses (mail or e-mail, depending on whether you're sending a printed or e-mailed invitation) almost always takes longer than you think. In some communities, e-mail has become such a prevalent mode of communication that a printed invitation might stand out and therefore get more attention. Another advantage of a mailed invitation is that you can include a reply card and envelope and ask people to send a contribution even if they cannot attend the party. But e-mailed invitations, using a Web site such as Evite.com, are gaining in popularity and are an inexpensive option for inviting people who can be easily reached by e-mail. In Chapter Five, Exhibit 5.1 provides some pros and cons to consider in deciding whether to use U.S. postal mail or e-mail.

Step 3: Prepare and Mail the Invitation

For invitations that will be printed and mailed by U.S. post, you will need the following materials:

- Invitation. Be clear on what the house party is for, the date and time, and that people should bring their checkbook. (See the sample invitations in Exhibit 8.1.)

- Reply card. Be sure to include clear ways for people to give even if they do not plan to come. "I can't come, but here's my contribution of $_____." (See the sample reply card in Exhibit 8.2.)

Exhibit 8.1
Sample House Party Invitation: GIFT

The Grassroots Institute for Fundraising Training (GIFT) develops and strengthens the grassroots fundraising skills of people working for social justice. GIFT helps organizations develop a broad base of individual donors to support their work. Its programs include a paid six-month internship for people of color, two-day fundraising workshops around the country, and a research project on fundraising and philanthropy in communities of color.

You are invited to a House Party to benefit GIFT: Grassroots Institute for Fundraising Training

You will:
- Munch on yummy refreshments
- Have scintillating conversations
- Learn the meaning of scintillating
- Meet GIFT graduates
- Learn about one of the most important groups we are involved with

Thursday, June 21st
6:00 – 8:00 pm

Jose and Julia's house
2345 First Street
Denver, CO

Please RSVP by June 14th

303-333-1234
or jose@igc.org

***Bring your questions
and your checkbook!***

Exhibit 8.2
Sample Reply Card: GIFT

_____ Yes, I'm coming to your GIFT house party! I'm bringing _____ additional guests.

_____ I'm sorry, I can't make it, but here's my contribution of

_____$25 _____ $50 _____ $100 $_____ (other)

Name_____

Address_____

City, State, ZIP_____

E-Mail_____

Phone_____

(Please make checks payable to GIFT and send to _Name, Address, City, State, ZIP._)

- Reply envelopes. These need to be small enough to fit inside the envelope carrying the invitation mailing. They will be used by people who are making a contribution even though they will not attend the party. Including this envelope increases the likelihood that people not coming will send in a donation.

- Larger envelopes for the mailing

- Stamps for the mailing

Mail out the invitations four to five weeks before the party is scheduled to take place.

If you want to explore sending invitations by e-mail, the information in Exhibit 8.3 will give you an idea of how that works.

Step 4: Make Follow-Up Calls

Phone calls will make or break a house party. Personal contact by the host is key to making sure people come. It is mainly the host's personal network that is being invited, and most people will come because they know and trust that person. In addition, people are busy and appreciate the reminder and personal touch of a

---
Exhibit 8.3

Sending Invitations by E-Mail or Evite.com

If you want to send your house party invitation by e-mail, you have two options. The first is to create a flyer and e-mail it as an attachment. The second is to use an online service such as Evite (www.evite.com), which is free. Go to their Web site for instructions on how to register and use their services. Be aware that like many free online services, their privacy policy indicates that they share your contact information (and sometimes other information too, such as sites you visit on the Internet) with other online businesses. If you're comfortable with that, they're a convenient and popular method of sending invitations by e-mail.

In either case, be sure there's a way for people to make a donation even if they can't come to the party. Be clear to whom checks should be made payable and where to send them, along with any other information you may require. Ideally, include an electronic version of the reply card for people to print out. If applicable, include a link to your Web site with information on your project or organization. If the site offers a way to donate online, be sure to highlight that in your invitation e-mail.

---

phone call. The host should begin making calls two to three weeks before the party is scheduled to take place.

People who cannot come should still be asked to give a donation. As much as half the money raised from the house party will come from these people if they are asked in the phone call. It's best to ask for a specific amount, saying something like, "I'm hoping you'll consider giving between $25 and $50 to this project." Then write down the amount people commit to on the House Party Tracking Sheet in Worksheet 8.1.

Handout 8.1 contains tips for making follow-up phone calls to encourage people to come to the house party.

In addition, Script 8.1 illustrates how to structure a follow-up call.

Worksheet 8.1
House Party Tracking Sheet

Use this worksheet to keep track of invitations mailed, follow-up calls made, and whether people are coming. If people are not coming, ask them for a donation and write their pledge in the appropriate column.

Name	Address	Phone	E-mail	Invitation sent	Calls	Coming?	Pledge	Received	Notes
Emetra Jones	123 Main St.	(601) 222-5353	none	Y 4/15	Y 5/1	N	$25	$25	Has mobility issues
Patrick Blackhawk	155 Broadway	(601) 222-1234		Y 4/15	Y 5/1	Y	$30	Will bring	Needs child care for kids 2 and 6

- Get to the point early on in the conversation: that you are calling to follow up on the house party invitation. Otherwise you'll find yourself tempted to have a long chat with your friend and then have a hard time bringing the conversation around to your fundraiser.

- Ask directly if your friend will come to your house party.

- If they cannot come, ask them if they can send in a contribution and mention a specific amount.

- After you ask for a commitment, be silent and wait for the answer. Avoid nervous chatter.

- Thank your friend for their time.

- Carefully record commitments.

Script 8.1
House Party Turnout Call Script

Structure of the call	What to say
Opening—you're calling people you know, so be yourself and chat. Be friendly, but make sure to move to the house party.	"Hi, Aunt Mamie, this is John. How are you?"
Tell them why you're calling: to follow up on the invitation to your house party.	"Good to hear. Well, as you know, I've been trying to buy a home here, and it's been hard to get loans, especially in my part of town near the reservation. In the process, I've learned through my work with a community group, South Dakotans United, that there is serious racism in the lending process. So I'm holding a house party to invite my friends and family to learn more and to raise money for South Dakotans United. Did you get my invitation?"
Remind them of the details: Tell them when and where the house party is and ask directly if they can come.	"Great. Well, the house party is on Sunday, August 10, from 4:00 to 6:00 in the afternoon. It will be a barbecue in my backyard and lots of the family will be there. We'll have a short program to explain what South Dakotans United is doing and then you'll have a chance to ask questions and make a donation. Can you join us?"
If they can't come, ask them to make a donation.	"Oh, I'm sorry that it's at the same time as your self-defense class. We'll miss you, but I'd like to ask if you can still make a contribution to South Dakotans United. Can you join us at $60?" (Be silent.) "You'd like to give $40? Great, I'll write that down. Thanks, Aunt Mamie, that will make a difference for the campaign. You can make your check payable to South Dakotans United and use the reply card and return envelope included in the invitation I sent you."
If they are planning to come, remind them of the logistics and to bring their checkbooks.	"Glad you can make it! Again, the barbeque will be from 4:00 to 6:00 in the afternoon; get here at 4:00 so you can catch the program. Be sure to bring your checkbook. Oh, and of course, feel free to bring any of your friends!"
Thank them!	"Thanks so much for your time, Aunt Mamie, and I'll look forward to seeing you there!"

Step 5: Prepare the Agenda, Practice the Pitch, and Hold the Party

It's important to plan the party, the presentation of your project, and especially the "pitch." The first thirty to forty-five minutes are for the guests to arrive, for people to socialize, munch on food, and check out any materials you have on display. The program should begin no more than an hour into the party. The following suggested program agenda will give you a sense of how the party will go.

SUGGESTED PROGRAM AGENDA (20–30 minutes)

(2–5 minutes—Host)	**Introduction:** Welcome and thank people for coming
(5 minutes—Host or other speaker)	**Why issue and project are important:** Interactive or dynamic presentation to illustrate what the problem is and why the issue you're working on is so compelling and urgent. Use stories to bring the issue to life.
(5 minutes—Host or other speaker)	**What impact this project will have:** What the project goals are, how this project will make a difference.
(5–10 minutes—Speaker continues in this role)	**Questions and Answers:** Provide an opportunity to engage the audience, answer questions, and have a more general discussion.
(5 minutes—Host)	**The Pitch:** Concrete ways their support can make a difference. How much you're trying to raise. Suggested amounts people should think about giving. After the pitch, give people time to write their checks and turn them in (see below).
(2 minutes—Host)	**Closing:** Thank everyone for coming and for their support. Invite them to continue eating and socializing.

The Pitch   The pitch should be timed to be at the peak of the program, right after the issue has been driven home or after a compelling story from a house party speaker. Use Resource D, Tips for Making a Pitch at an Event, to get ideas for doing the pitch.

Immediately after the host makes the pitch, pass envelopes around to everyone in the room with a contribution slip that tells people how to make the check out or how to give with a credit card, if available, and asks for people's contact information (you can use the same reply slip that you included in the mailing). Make sure everyone has a pen and give them a few minutes to write their checks. Then approach them with a basket to collect the contributions. It is much more effective to have someone personally approach people with a basket than to pass the basket around or leave it on a table. This way, guests will more likely each make a contribution and will know exactly what to do with it.

Be sure to include an option on the contribution slip for people to make a pledge. Some people will be so moved by the presentation that they decide they want to give a larger amount than they brought with them; others may not have brought their checkbook or can't give right away.

Ask everyone to fill out the contribution slip and include their contact information and the amount they are giving so that you have a record of who gave what amount. Checks often include people's contact information, but sometimes the contact information is old, and sometimes people give cash and you'll want to have a record of who gave it. This is important so that you can thank people and so that you can keep good records for your organization.

Here is one of the most important details: The house party host needs to make a monetary donation. Certainly, hosting the house party is a major contribution. However, for the guests to give money, it is important that the host be able to say that she gives money and wants her friends to join her.

A note about donations to political campaigns. If your house party is raising funds for a political campaign, keep in mind that donations to political electoral campaigns have strict reporting laws, so check the laws of your state and region. The Federal Political Practices Commission requires that donors who give more than $250 over the course of an election cycle must inform the commission of their employer and occupation. Political donations are not tax-deductible.

Food and Drink   Refreshments at the house party can be as plain or fancy as you'd like. The important thing is to have something for people to nibble on. The host should serve whatever they would like and whatever fits in their budget. If they feel comfortable doing this, they can ask some of the people coming to the house party to bring food and drink to share. This can improve their commitment to come, but don't let them think this is their contribution to the fundraising effort. If there is time to solicit favorite local restaurants or stores to donate food, this will help offset the cost.

Materials   Assemble the following materials to have at the party:

- Contribution envelopes, contribution slips, and a basket to collect contributions and pledges.
- Informational flyers, brochures, posters, photos, and so on, to give people a flavor of what the organization does and the issue the house party is spotlighting. Some materials can be for display only, such as photos, and some materials you should give away to guests.
- If you have sales items such as T-shirts, buttons, books, videos, and so on, have some available to sell to guests.

Step 6: Send Thank-Yous

Within a week of the house party, thank-you notes should go out to everyone who made a contribution, either at the party or through the mail. The host can either sign the project's thank-you notes or write separate ones. It's nice to have the personal touch of a thank-you from the host, but if the project is an ongoing one, it is also important for the project or organization to begin developing a connection and relationship directly with the donor.

Step 7: Evaluate the Event

Evaluate how the house party went so you can learn from your experience and pass it on to others who may want to do a house party. What went well? What was challenging? How many people came and how much money did you raise at the party? How much money did you raise from people who did not come? Did you learn anything that you'd like to pass on to the next house party host or to the organization? Would you feel comfortable coaching someone else to do a house party?

VARIATION ON A THEME: A "VIRTUAL HOUSE PARTY"

While nothing beats asking people in person, not everyone is in a position to hold a house party. The next best thing is to have a virtual house party, a party that doesn't actually happen at a real place or time. Instead, it happens by way of a letter that describes an imaginary account of what an actual house party would be like if you were holding one and asks the recipient to make a donation without the bother of coming to a party.

Five Steps to a "Virtual House Party"

1. *The Letter.* Compose a letter that describes your house party, tells about the project or cause, and asks for donations. When describing your house party, you can be as imaginative and humorous as you want.

2. *The Guest List.* Brainstorm a list of people you want to "invite." (See Resource B, Who Can You Ask?) Don't be shy about including as many people as you can on your list.

3. *The Mailing.* Make as many copies of the letter as you need. Personalize each letter. Send it via e-mail as described earlier in this chapter or via regular mail with a return donor envelope and a pledge form. If possible, make phone calls to follow up on the letter, as the calls can double the amount you raise.

4. *The Money.* As each donation is received, keep careful records of the donor and the amount.

5. *The Thank-You.* Send out prompt, personal, hand-written notes to all donors. Let them know how much their contribution is appreciated.

Here's a sample virtual house party letter written by Terry Keleher, volunteer with Californians for Justice, about an initiative on the California ballot in 1996.

Dear Friend,

Imagine, for a moment, being in my living room next Friday evening. My apartment in Oakland is cozy and colorful, filled with strange art objects I've made or collected, a wide assortment of books and musical instruments, and a motley array of second-hand furniture. It's not real fancy or big in size, but there's character, warmth, and comfort to it. Also imagine that you're surrounded by a roomful of interesting and extraordinary people, much like yourself. They're smart, humorous, creative folks who share many of your world views and political values.

Furthermore, imagine that I've stretched my Irish-Italian hospitality to its outermost limits, serving scrumptious hors d'oeuvres and refreshments, including fresh, homemade soda bread and biscotti still warm from the oven, rich chocolate desserts teasingly waiting to be devoured, along with plentiful supplies of hot beverages and other fine brews.

This would be the setting if I were holding a campaign "house party," where people gather at the home of someone they know to socialize, enjoy tasty refreshments, and learn about how they can support a current political campaign.

But I'm not holding a conventional house party. My apartment is too small to accommodate all the people I would want there, and besides, many of them live much too far away. Instead, I'm holding a "virtual house party," a high-tech creature of my own invention, which I am piloting with this letter.

So whether you're a blood relative, a friend I hold in high regard even if we haven't been in touch lately, or someone I see on a regular basis, I wouldn't want to snub you by leaving you off the invitation list and deny you the opportunity to be a part of this way-cool, definitely hip, trend-setting historic affair.

Any effective house party, actual or virtual, includes a presentation about a cause or project, followed by a "pitch"—a request for financial support—and volunteer help. Of course, I would let you know this in advance so you could come prepared and maybe even bring a friend.

So, getting back to my living room on Friday evening, imagine yourself sitting back and listening intently to what I would have to say:

Over the past year, I've been volunteering my time on an important political campaign going on in California. It's an effort to save affirmative action programs, now being attacked by conservative forces by way of a statewide ballot initiative that will be voted on in November. It's a deceptive initiative titled the "California Civil Rights Initiative" when it's just the opposite. This is an election issue designed to tap into people's racism and economic anxieties.

Fortunately, this campaign offers us a real opportunity to fight back and raise the issues. During this election, we began forming a new organization, Californians for Justice (CFJ), to fight these sorts of right-wing initiatives in the short term and build a lasting progressive organization that will work for social, racial, and economic justice over the long haul.

Our goal is to raise $180,000 so CFJ can conduct a field campaign in 1,500 targeted precincts. This is an ambitious but possible goal. It costs the campaign approximately $120 to operate in each precinct. I'd like to ask you to help by making a donation to this effort. You can choose to adopt a precinct with a contribution of $120, or you can adopt half a precinct for $60. Picture all the thousands of CFJ volunteers and members who are knocking on doors as we speak. Please dig deep, and make this *the biggest contribution you'll make this election season.*

So now you've heard the pitch. It's time for me to close and let you decide if you can help. Afterward, the virtual house party continues with all its fine company, conversation, and confections. I hope you've enjoyed being one of my "guests." And I hope you can help me make this experiment as successful as possible.

I won't actually see you on Friday night. But I hope you'll consider making a generous gift. It will make a big difference in our work. I hope all is well with you and please know that you have a standing invitation to come over for a real visit any time you get the chance. I'll be thinking of you Friday and on Election Day, and I'll save some dessert for you.

Virtually yours,

Terry Keleher

WORKPLAN

The following workplan provides a summary of the key steps necessary to implement this fundraising strategy and an estimated time frame for each step. It is meant to be a template from which to create your own plan and your own timeline. By taking the time to create a plan and timeline, you'll be more organized, more likely to avoid last-minute crises, and ultimately more successful in raising the money you need.

Workplan 8.1
House Party

What	Who	When (Week Number)						Done
		1	2	3	4	5	6	
1. Find a host and make a plan								
Recruit hosts		x						
Choose date, time, and location of house party		x						
Make a workplan and budget		x						
2. Prepare an invitation list								
Brainstorm as large an invitation list as possible		x						
Track down e-mails and addresses for invitees		x	x	x				
3. Prepare and send the invitation materials								
Prepare invitation and reply slip			x					
Mail invitations			x	x				
4. Make follow-up calls								
Make calls to confirm attendees, ask others to still give						x	x	
Two days before house party, make reminder calls							x	
5. Prepare the agenda, practice the pitch, and hold the party								
Prepare program and pitch					x	x		
Gather the materials needed for the party					x	x	x	
Buy and prepare food and refreshments							x	
Hold the party							x	
6. Send thank-yous							x	
7. Evaluate							x	

Community Dinners

People love to eat and socialize, and many successful fundraisers can be held as a variation on a food theme: a cocktail party, an intimate dinner party at someone's home, or a larger community dinner. This chapter focuses on how to hold a community dinner. Fundraising dinners take advantage of the human desire to come together, have fun, feel part of a community, and support a good cause. A community dinner is usually held in a public venue such as a community center, restaurant, hotel, or other public space. During the dinner, people mingle, catch up with old acquaintances, meet new people, and learn about the cause or organization. There is usually a program that may honor someone and include an emcee, speakers, entertainment, and a fundraising pitch. There may be additional fundraising events within the dinner framework, such as a silent auction, ad book, or raffle (described in Chapters Eleven, Twelve, and Fourteen), which can help raise extra funds.

In this chapter we focus on a local, grassroots dinner as opposed to a high-priced special event that often requires a professional event planner or the time of the organization's staff. Some of the same principles apply whether you host a larger, more expensive event or a smaller community dinner, but given the focus of this book, we concentrate here on how to keep overhead costs down and how volunteers can run such a dinner.

BEST USES

Dinners are a great fundraising activity if you are trying to do any of the following:

- Raise the visibility of your project.
- Build community, celebrate accomplishments, deepen relationships with and the commitment of people who have already been involved with your project (as volunteers, donors, or supporters). This relationship building can strengthen other aspects of your project as well as future potential fundraising work.

- Bring in new money from new people.

- Provide a way for volunteers to learn new skills and get more comfortable with fundraising activities.

Raising large amounts of money is usually not the immediate, primary goal of most dinners, since there are faster ways of raising money in the short term and dinners take a lot of work. However, if you are trying to establish your project and you have other community-building goals, dinners can be a great way to go.

THINGS TO CONSIDER

Dinners take a fair amount of work and attention to detail. Before taking on a dinner, consider whether you have enough enthusiastic volunteers to help carry out the event. Depending on how large your dinner will be, it is good to have a core, committed group of about three to five coordinators and a wider pool of at least another five to ten volunteers. It can be helpful if one of the dinner coordinators has had experience organizing some kind of event, such as a wedding or commitment ceremony, a family reunion, a big birthday party, or something comparable that would have given them an appreciation for the details and deadlines this kind of undertaking involves.

A successful dinner takes at least three months to organize; six months is ideal. So again, if your project needs money more quickly and doesn't have much up-front money to put into a dinner (see "Costs"), you might want to do a house party or direct personal asks. However, if you have other goals such as those listed above, a dinner might be the perfect event for you. You may be organizing a dinner as a one-time event, but as with many fundraising strategies, if you can repeat the event year after year, it will become easier and easier to organize (particularly if you evaluate what went well and what areas to improve and keep good records). In addition, you should be able to increase your financial returns from the event each year. Many organizations hold annual dinners, and those that do have found that it takes two or three years for the event to smooth out kinks, to build a loyal base of attendees, and to develop a "tradition" status. Once the event has been established as a successful affair, a segment of your supporters are likely to return year after year. Some will bring their friends, so that new people are introduced to your project. If you follow the steps outlined in this chapter, you can both energize your supporters and make a modest amount of money.

COSTS

The costs for a dinner can be kept lower if many of the following items are donated:

- Venue for the event
- Tables and chairs
- Food and drink
- Paper goods or place settings
- Equipment (such as a sound system)
- Insurance (liability insurance is sometimes required by the venue)
- Fees and expenses for entertainers or guest speakers
- Child care
- Invitation design, printing, postage
- Publicity (ads, public service announcements, flyers)
- Copying of materials
- Postage for thank-you letters

STEPS TO TAKE

These are the steps you should plan on taking. Each will be discussed in detail.

1. Make a plan and budget
2. Recruit volunteers
3. Develop invitation list
4. Find dinner site and set date
5. Design, print, and send invitations
6. Plan program
7. Arrange food, drink, and other logistics
8. Publicize event, do turnout calls, sell tickets
9. Review event details and hold the event
10. Evaluate the event and send thank-yous

As you go through the steps in detail, use the sample workplan at the end of the chapter to create a timeline and task list.

Step 1: Make a Plan and Budget

Because a dinner is a larger event than most, the core group of three to five coordinators should help set the goals for the dinner, make a workplan and budget, and recruit and coordinate the other volunteers who will help carry out all the tasks that are needed for the dinner. Use the Community Dinner Planning Worksheet (Worksheet 9.1) to help you and the coordinators think through your goals and plan.

The coordinating committee should be clear about the goals for the dinner—fundraising and others—and what resources you have. It's easy for people to get swept up into fantasies of what famous person would be great to perform at the event, what kind of food you want, and so on. Setting realistic goals will help you avoid planning an event that loses money and that doesn't attract the guests you had hoped would attend.

Think about other ways to raise money at the dinner. For example, at any dinner, entrance fees and tickets alone may not raise the funds you need or tap into the giving potential of the people who attend. You may want to add a pitch, where someone gives a moving and often personal presentation of why the issue and the work are so important and asks the guests to consider making an additional contribution. At that point, envelopes are provided for people to make their donations.

Dinners are versatile because other forms of fundraising can be easily built into the event, such as the following:

- Raffles
- Silent auctions
- Program ad books
- Dinner sponsorship
- Table sponsors

Later chapters describe raffles, auctions, and ad books in detail; we discuss sponsorships in this chapter. These extra fundraising activities also allow you to get support from people who may not attend the event but who want to contribute. That means that you should sell raffle tickets and ad space far before the actual dinner to reach the fundraising potential of these extra activities. These strategies are a perfect project for a subcommittee of volunteers to coordinate. Make sure that there is good communication among the committees organizing these auxiliary fundraising strategies and the volunteers who are soliciting sponsorships and other in-kind items for the dinner so that the same vendors or people are not being asked twice for donations related to the same event.

Decide if you want a host committee or sponsors for the event. A host committee is usually made up of visible members of the community who are willing to lend their name to show that the dinner and your organization are widely supported. Try to recruit a host committee early on in the process so that the committee names can be printed on the invitation. Usually, committee members are asked to make a financial contribution to the dinner and, even if they aren't able to attend, to send invitations to their friends.

Dinner sponsorship is a way to get individuals, organizations, and businesses to give a substantial donation or even to underwrite the dinner. In return, the sponsors' names are featured prominently in the invitations, on programs, and at the event itself through banners or displays. Depending on your project, you may need to think through which businesses might be appropriate sponsors and which ones would hurt your organization's image. For example, if you are working on environmental issues, sponsorship by a company known to pollute the air in your community would likely alienate your supporters. On the other hand, some businesses may genuinely support your cause and it might serve both your interests to include them as prospective sponsors.

Another way to get donations is through table sponsorships. Organizations or individuals who agree to sponsor a table pay a lump sum—usually more than the actual cost of the total number of seats at the table—and then give tickets to people within their organization or to friends.

The key to a successful dinner is good planning. Creating a detailed workplan on the front end will help save much headache in the long run. Because teamwork done mainly by volunteers is so important to successful dinners, it is imperative that your workplan specify the point person and other volunteers for each task or series of related tasks. Include deadlines that give enough cushion to allow for delays or problems that may come up. Even then, expect some crisis, such as a speaker or performer who gets sick the day before the event or a printing error that advertises the wrong date for the event. (Review Chapter Two, Building Your Fundraising Team, for more tips on how to build and work with your volunteer team.)

Plan to organize your volunteers into committees to carry out the range of tasks required. You might have a committee that works on the program—speakers, location, food, and so on; another committee that works on the invitation and publicity to get people to attend; and a committee that figures out ways to increase the money raised by producing an ad book, raffle, or silent auction. The core planning committee should develop the overall workplan that sets goals, parameters, and as much detail as possible for the project committees. Generally, it is better to err on the side of more detail rather than less, since it is better to have a conversation on the front end about differing approaches than after something has been implemented in a different way than envisioned. For example, if you are part of an immigrant parent network that is planning a large dinner, don't send the program committee off to figure out who the entertainers and speakers will be without defining some parameters. If the vision of the core committee is for the program to have community members perform and be the key speakers, the program committee needs to know that so that it doesn't go off and recruit the local, flashy politician who is a good speaker but does not represent the values of the immigrant parent network.

To decide whether a dinner is the right event for your group, consult Worksheet 9.1.

Step 2: Recruit Volunteers

Dinners depend on the enthusiasm and commitment of volunteers. A dinner can be a nice entry point for someone to learn how to do fundraising, find out more about the project, and become invested in the future of the project. The skills one needs for putting together a dinner can translate very well to other work your project does, such as planning a speaking event, organizing a rally, recruiting people to a public meeting to make demands of a decision maker, and so forth.

Here are some ideas of what volunteers can do:

- Find dinner venue
- Send invitations to and follow up with their friends, family, and networks
- Solicit sponsorships
- Sell tickets to the dinner
- Make food
- Help with room setup and cleanup
- Recruit performers and speakers
- Be a performer or speaker

Use this worksheet with your dinner planning team to come up with fundraising goals, goals besides raising money, and resources. Then use the steps in the chapter and sample workplan to make a detailed plan.

What are our fundraising goals?

- Fundraising goal $ _5000_ – Costs $ _1500_ = Total (NET) $ _3500_

- How can we raise money from people/places that would not give otherwise?

  Table sponsorships—arts collectives, local businesses, city arts commission, etc.

  New donors—who have been to arts expo but haven't given $ yet

- Can we get in-kind donations for the event?

  Yes. Ask Rosi's Diner, Taqueria Cancun, JJ's Café. Brainstorm w/ volunteers.

- In addition to ticket sales, what are other ways to raise money at the dinner?

  ☐ Do pitch   ☐ Raffle   ☐ Ad book   ☐ Table sponsorship

  ☐ Silent auction   ☐ Other   _sponsor others to come_

  Do silent auction—we have a lot of artists who can donate work. Ad book too time consuming for us. Instead of raffle, ask people who can't come to sponsor others.

What are our goals besides raising money? Do we want to:

- Increase our project's visibility? Celebrate victories? Thank and motivate people?

- Increase volunteer commitment, fundraising skills, other skills?

  —Arts expo is in 6 months—we want to increase visibility of our arts group.

  —Need volunteers to plan arts expo—recruit 15 volunteers to help plan dinner so that at least 5 can help with expo. Especially train on fundraising.

  —Need artist submissions—insert call for art submissions into dinner invitation.

What resources do we have?

- How much money do we have up front? *$500—need another $1000*

- Who can we ask for money?

  We have a list of 600 people who have attended our arts expos in the last 3 years. Our dinner and arts expo planning teams should also brainstorm lists of others we should invite.

- How much time to we have to plan the event? _3 months_

- Who can we recruit to help plan and run the event?

  50 past volunteers from last year's expo, but haven't been in touch with them. Call & recruit them to help with dinner and tell them this is to raise money for this year's arts expo.

- Other resources: _Artists who can donate work_

- Make the fundraising pitch
- Collect donations after the pitch
- Write thank-you letters to people who give money

See Resource A, Volunteer Recruitment Form, for help with recruiting volunteers. Once you have your volunteer crew, turn your attention to training and supporting them and being thoughtful about how they like to work and how they can plug in. Troubleshoot if problems arise. It's useful to have benchmarks in your workplan to measure how progress is going and to help adjust plans if needed.

Step 3: Develop Invitation List

With your volunteers, brainstorm a list of friends, family, coworkers, neighbors, and acquaintances who might be interested in learning more about your project and who might enjoy coming to a dinner. (Use Resource B, Who Can You Ask? to help brainstorm whom to invite.) You'll need to send invitations to at least two hundred or three hundred people if you want fifty people to come to your dinner. You may want to invite people who live in another state or who for some other reason cannot attend but may be willing to make a contribution anyway.

Step 4: Find a Dinner Site, Set the Date and Time

Try to get the space for your dinner donated or rented to you at a low rate. Especially if this is the first dinner you are organizing, it is not wise to be investing a lot of money on the front end. If you can be flexible about the date of your event, there might be more opportunities for free or low-cost spaces.

Consider a location that your supporters will find convenient and comfortable. If you are a project that works on women's issues, see if there are any women's centers or YWCAs. If you are a project based in the Latino or Asian community, try to find a space within that community. If you are a multiracial organization, try to find a space that is somewhat neutral or one where a variety of communities will feel comfortable. As soon as you set a date, send out a "Save the Date" e-mail or postcard to your closest supporters and your volunteers.

Think about all the arrangements that you will need to make for the dinner and what types of facilities will be required. Some considerations might be the following:

- Will you need a kitchen to heat up donated food or where volunteers can cook the dinner?

- Do you need to provide child care? If so, have a child-friendly room nearby, rather than just a corner in the main room, so that the kids can play without disrupting the program.

- Do you need an accessible space? Even if you are not sure you need it, it is always good to plan your event in a place accessible to people with disabilities. This sends a message that everyone in the community is welcome.

- Are there are enough tables and chairs for your event, or do you need to borrow some?

- Does the place already have a sound system or will you need to borrow or rent one?

- Does the venue require you to have liability insurance?

If liability insurance is required, you have a couple of options, depending on your group. If you are an established nonprofit organization with an office, you might already have a policy for liability insurance to which you can add a rider that covers you for the day of the event. If you are an all-volunteer group that is not part of a nonprofit organization, you can sometimes get coverage for liability insurance by using the homeowner's insurance policy of one of the members of your group. Check with the person's insurance company. If no one owns a home, find out if the venue itself can cover you under their liability insurance, even if it means charging you something for that coverage.

Step 5: Design, Print, and Send Invitations

The invitations can be as simple or as fancy as you like and can afford. If you have a volunteer with design skills, this is the time to let them shine! Just be sure to include the key logistical details in the invitation: what, where, when, directions to the dinner, number or e-mail to reply. Include a reply card and envelope so that if people can't come to the event, they can still make a donation. If you have decided on a speaker, performer, or honoree, include this on the invitation. A critical step is to have several people proofread the invitation before it is printed.

Have a mailing party with volunteers to get the invitations out. Mailings are a great way for volunteers to get to know each other, learn more about the project, and help get some concrete work done. If you have the capacity, it is very helpful to ask volunteers to write a note on the invitations to add a special personal touch. Exhibit 9.1 shows an invitation and reply form simply designed for a local community service project.

Step 6: Plan the Program

The program is where you introduce your project's mission and accomplishments. You can include one or two speakers who are inspirational, represent your project, and can connect with your audience. Ideally, someone has seen them speak before or can work with them to prepare a concise, lively talk.

The program is also an opportunity to have performers who will resonate with your audience and convey the image and values of your project. Again, it's ideal if one of your volunteers or coordinating committee members has seen the performer and can attest that they are a good fit for your project and dinner. Too many people have been to an event where the performer was painfully unprepared or they were not a good fit for the audience. Mimi was once at a volunteer appreciation and fundraising party for a group that was working to increase the vote in low-income communities of color. The dinner organizers, all people of color, knew that most of the people coming would be people of color and primarily African American. However, they failed to think about what *generation* of people would be coming. A well-respected, talented African-American a capella folk group performed some classic songs from the 1960s, but a significant part of the audience—young African Americans, Latinos, and Asian Americans—listened politely, then left the event early. Clearly, the performers were not the right choice for this audience.

These days, people also use e-mail and an e-mail invitation service such as Evite to invite people to parties. Evite and other similar programs are Web-based invitation services that allow a host to design their own invitation, enter their invitees' e-mail addresses, and track replies online. You can even set it up so that reminder e-mails go out a couple days before your event. See Exhibit 8.3 in Chapter Eight for a detailed discussion of how to send e-mailed invitations, and Exhibit 5.1 in Chapter Five for the pros and cons of using U.S. postal mail versus e-mail.

The emcee can make or break a dinner. Think about the tone you want to convey at your dinner and choose an emcee to match that tone. If you want your event to be solemn and inspirational, don't choose your friend the aspiring comedian. If you want your emcee to be snappy and to move the program along, don't choose

Exhibit 9.1
Sample Community Dinner Invitation (Outside)

People of Progress 1242 Center Street, Redding, CA 96001   530 243-3811
www.peopleofprogress.org

Potato Ice Cream

Sweet Potato Pie

Green Salad

Roasted Rosemary New Potatoes

Roasted Chicken

Shasta County Contest-winning Potato Salad

Potato Chips & Dip

People of Progress

OC***TUBER***FEST

ANNUAL DINNER & GIFT BASKET AUCTION

Exhibit 9.1 *(continued)*
Sample Community Dinner Invitation (Inside)

Our community has been able to depend upon
People of Progress for 31 years.
Please help us continue this work
and join us for this year's dinner.
Octuberfest honors people, potatoes, and our ability
to move forward together despite adversity.

THIS YEAR'S OCTUBERFEST FEATURES:

A PRODIGIOUS POTATO INSPIRED REPAST*

GIFT BASKET AUCTION

SHASTA COUNTY'S BEST POTATO JOKE

POTATO ENTERTAINMENT

SHASTA COUNTY'S BEST POTATO SALAD

AND OUR OWN POTATO ICE CREAM!

— — — — — — — — — — — —

Friday, October 29, 2003
6:00 p.m. $15 per person
(children 8 and under, $8.00)
First United Methodist Church Social Hall
(corner of South & East Streets, enter from rear of building)

Call P.O.P. at 243-3811 to reserve your spuds
or return the enclosed reservation card.

People of Progress helps over 16,000 people annually with food for over 190,000 meals,
1,800 bus passes, 400 voice mail boxes, 9,000 emergency clothing items,
2 community gardens, rent assistance, disaster response, and information/referrals
along with emergency client casework and advocacy.
We participate in and/or lead many collaborative projects and efforts on
homelessness, housing, motels and nutrition.
•
Potatoes have long been important for anyone living on a modest food budget.
Potatoes originated in the New World where there were dozens of varieties in many colors,
shapes and flavors suited to grow in a wide variety of soils and climates.
Throughout history, many cultures have been sustained by the sturdy spud.

* *Carbivores, Low-Carbivores, Carnivores and Herbivores are welcome. Dinner menu on back.*

Exhibit 9.1 *(continued)*

Sample Community Dinner Invitation (Reply Card)

PEOPLE OF PROGRESS

OC*TUBER*FEST

___ *Yes! I'm coming! Please reserve* ____ *spud dinners @ $15*

Children 8 and under, $8.00

___ *Nope. Can't make it, but here's my contribution.*

Tater Tot Level $5	*Hash Brown Level $10*	*French Fry Level $25*
Curley Fry Level $35	*Mashed Potato Level $50*	*Baked Potato Level $75*
Scalloped Potato Level $100	*Cajun Level $500*	*Roasted Garlic Mashed Potato Level $1,000*

Total enclosed: $ _____ Tickets will be held for you at the door

You are also welcome to phone in your reservation, then pay at the door. 243-3811

Name: _____ Phone: _____

Address: _____

City: _____ Zip: _____

---

the wonderful but long-winded community activist who always tells stories of how things were back in their day. Someone from your coordinating committee should prepare the emcee by being clear about the tone you are trying to convey, familiarizing them with the program and the flow of the room, and conveying any talking points they want them to use. Make sure your emcee has a written, detailed agenda, including any bios for performers and pronunciation keys for difficult names. Plan to have someone from the coordinating committee near the stage during the program in case the emcee has questions or unforeseen things come up, such as a performer who arrives late or the need for last-minute logistical announcements.

Step 7: Arrange Food, Drink, and Other Logistics

Good food—and enough of it—is very important to the success of the event. People who are happy and full are much more likely to give money and walk away with a positive feeling about the evening and your project than people who are still hungry at the end of the meal. So do not skimp on the food!

As with other items for the dinner, the more you can get donated, the better.

- Make a list of restaurants that you and other volunteers frequent. It is much easier to get a food donation from a restaurant that recognizes that you are a regular customer.

- Call and, if possible, visit the restaurants in person. Introduce yourself and your project, ask who you should speak to about making donations, and get a firm commitment for a donation or at least a clear notion about how to follow up.

- Leave a simple letter explaining your project, the purpose, date, and time of your event, and clearly asking for a food donation for the event.

- Be sure to tell them if you will display the name of their restaurant at the dinner, give them recognition in the program, and any other ways their restaurant will get good publicity.

- Some grocery stores will also donate food and drinks. If you are considering serving alcohol, find out if the venue allows it and if you need a liquor license.

It is useful to develop a plan showing a minute-by-minute flow of the dinner at least a week or two before the event. This helps everyone picture the event, identify things that haven't yet been taken care of, and clarify roles needed for the day. You may want to get each of your committees to draw up a detailed plan for each of their pieces and then create a master plan for the flow of the dinner. Be as detailed as you possibly can. Here are some examples of things to include:

- Where will people park?

- How is the food arriving at the site? Is it being delivered? By whom? Is it being picked up? By whom?

- Will food need to be reheated? Where and by whom? Does the food need to be kept warm? How will that happen?

- How will registration happen? What lists need to be printed beforehand and containing what kind of information? How will volunteers get the lists they need? What will happen with people who arrive who have not bought tickets yet?

- Who is working with the emcee? Who is the timer for the speakers? Who will be managing the performers or speakers?

- Who is doing the pitch? Who will be going around the room to collect donations?

By thinking through these details ahead of time, you can readjust the flow of the dinner plan if needed. You will also have enough time to recruit volunteers and prepare people who have roles during the event, such as your speakers, master of ceremonies, auctioneer, and so on.

When writing the minute-by-minute plan for the event, include the logistics and schedule for food donation pickups.

Volunteers can also donate food (cooked or just ingredients) and drinks to the event. Or the dinner can be a potluck—a good way for volunteers to participate and share. Another option is for a committee of cooks to have a food budget and cook the meal. In that case, be sure that the cooks have the appropriate facilities in which to cook and heat up food.

Have a place on the reply form to indicate whether child care is needed and for what ages of children; ask volunteers doing turnout calls also to ask about child care needs and the children's ages.

Some other considerations: Who will unlock and lock the dinner venue? Where do you put the trash at the end of the night? The more you plan ahead and make these arrangements, the smoother your evening will go.

Step 8: Publicize the Event, Make Turnout Calls, and Encourage Early Donations

Publicize your event. Aside from the formal invitation, you can publicize the event more broadly. If e-mail works for the community you are inviting, design a simple e-mail message that explains your cause, makes the event look appealing, gives clear logistics, and indicates an easy way to reply. Forward this announcement to appropriate lists and encourage others to forward it as well. You may want to publicize the dinner in such places as the local newspaper; some radio stations will allow you to do a public service announcement about the dinner and your project. You can post flyers in the communities you work in and with organizations you know. Always keep in mind, however, that the personal contact of a phone call is the most effective way to get people to turn out to any event.

Make turnout calls. This is one of the most important steps. There is no use in having a fantastic program, the best raffle items, and delicious food if people don't actually come to the event. The most effective way to make sure people come is to make follow-up phone calls to the people who received invitations. The personal contact of a call can make your dinner stand out, help someone understand your project better, and allow you to count on at least a certain number of people coming to the dinner. People are much more likely to attend if they actually purchase their ticket ahead of time, so as much as possible, encourage the person to send in their reply along with a check.

The goal of turnout phone calls is to get the dinner on people's radar screen, get people to commit to coming to the dinner, ask people to pay for and send in the money for their tickets ahead of time, and get a sense of how many people will be coming. Even if you make turnout calls a couple of weeks in advance, some people will wait to buy tickets until the last few days before the event, and others will just show up on the evening of the dinner. It is important nonetheless for you to estimate how many people you think may be coming so that you can have the right amount of food.

Another important goal of the phone call is to ask people who will not be able to come to the dinner to make a contribution nonetheless. You can ask them to sponsor other community members to attend the dinner or to make a straightforward contribution. Handout 9.1 has five tips to keep in mind as you make the phone calls.

Here's an example of a call following up on a dinner invitation:

Janet: Hi, my name is Janet and I'm a parent with Schools for All Tennesseans, SAT. May I please speak to Dennis?

Dennis: This is Dennis.

Janet: Hi, Dennis. As you may know, next month is the anniversary of the Supreme Court decision in *Brown* v. *Board of Education* essentially outlawing segregation in schools. SAT is hosting a celebration and fundraising dinner at Jefferson Elementary School. Did you get our invitation?

Dennis: Yes, I think I received something in the mail through the PTA.

Janet: Great! So you have kids who go to Jefferson?

Dennis: Two of them.

Janet: Well, then you know that the school is cutting after-school programs, which makes it real hard for parents who have to work.

Dennis: Yeah, I'm not sure what to do with mine.

Janet: Well, SAT is going to the school board to give them a piece of our mind, but we need community members to join us and also to come out

- Be friendly; introduce yourself and explain why you're calling.

- Ask directly if people will come to the dinner.

- If they can attend, sign them up and ask them to send their reply form and check.

- If they cannot come, ask them to make a contribution to the project.

- After you ask for a commitment, be silent and wait for their answer. Don't fill in with nervous chatter.

- Carefully record commitments—dinner reply and pledge.

to our fundraising dinner. Our dinner is on Saturday, May 15, from 5:00 to 7:00 P.M. at Jefferson. Should be a lot of fun. Can you join us?

Dennis: Saturday, hmm. I think we can do it. Sure.

Janet: Great, I'll sign you up right now. How many people from your family should I sign up?

Dennis: Me, my two kids, and their grandmother.

Janet: OK, that's four seats. Tickets are $25 for each adult and $5 for kids, so that totals $60. Will you be paying that by check?

Dennis: Well, that's a lot.

Janet: Yes it is; we're investing in our kids' programs and future.

Dennis: Well, I suppose I can do that. I'll pay when we get there.

Janet: Actually, it helps us a lot in our preparations if you could send your check ahead of time in that reply envelope that you got with the invitation. Could you do that for us?

Dennis: Well, I suppose I can.

Janet: Great! It was nice speaking with you and thank you for your time! I look forward to meeting you. See you at the celebration on Saturday, May 15!

Dennis: See you then. And thank you for all your work.

If Dennis can't come to the dinner, Janet asks him to donate anyway:

Dennis: No, I'm sorry, May 15th is my mother's birthday and we're all going out to dinner.

Janet: Oh, I'm sorry that you can't join us. We'd love to have you there in spirit anyway. You can sponsor two community members to join us that night. Tickets are $25 each. Could you sponsor two community members at $50?

Dennis: Where did you learn that? That's pretty smart. Well, I don't think I can do $50 but I'll do one ticket at $25.

Janet: Thanks, that would be great. I'll write that down. You can send your check in the reply envelope that came with the invitation we sent you. On the reply card, there's a place to check off that you'd like to sponsor someone to attend. Can we call you when we speak at the school board?

Dennis: Definitely. I'd like to give them a piece of my mind, too. . . .

Janet: OK, we'll call you. Have a nice birthday celebration! Good night!

To ensure the absolute best turnout, you could make a round of reminder calls to everyone who has sent in their reply cards with reservations for the dinner. Keep it short and simple. Tell them you're making sure they have the details—the specific time, logistics, and any tips on things like where to park.

Use the tracking sheet in Worksheet 9.2 to keep track of who you sent invitations to, your follow-up calls, who will be coming, how much money they commit to giving, and whether their donation has been received.

Step 9: Review Event Details and Hold the Event

Materials   Make a checklist of all the materials you need for the event itself. Double- and triple-check the list before the event. Here are some of the items you may need:

- ☐ Guest lists (make several extra copies) with indications for who has replied, who has prepaid
- ☐ Cash and change for ticket purchases
- ☐ Pens for registration and writing checks
- ☐ Signs to direct people (to the restrooms, to the coat room, to child care, and so on)
- ☐ Tables and chairs
- ☐ Scissors, stapler, and tape (duct and Scotch)
- ☐ Flyers and other informational materials about the issue and project
- ☐ Markers: regular and permanent (in case you have to make signs for outside)
- ☐ Name tags
- ☐ Reply envelopes, contribution cards, and baskets for collecting donations after the pitch
- ☐ Eating utensils, plates, napkins
- ☐ Decorations
- ☐ Ladder to help hang things up
- ☐ Other _____

Worksheet 9.2
Dinner Invitation, Turnout, and Donation Tracking

Use this worksheet to keep track of invitations mailed, follow-up calls made, and whether people are coming. If people are not coming, ask them for a donation and write their pledge in the appropriate column.

Name	Address	Phone	E-mail	Invitation sent	Calls	Coming?	Pledge	Received	Notes
Ernest Mark	15 Fifth Ave.	(601) 222-5353	none	7/17	7/28	N	$50	8/12	
Manami Kano	316 Aspen	(601) 222-1234	mk@yahoo.com	7/17	8/1	Y			

Human Traffic   Plan the physical layout of the event space and how people will move around the space. Where will people register? Plan to set up the registration table so that everyone arriving has to sign in and pay for their tickets if they have not already done so, and make sure there is enough room for people who are waiting to register.

Where will people mingle before the dinner? Is this a sit-down or a buffet dinner? If it is a buffet dinner, how do you want people to line up and get the food? This can take a lot of time if not done right. Do you want to call people one table at a time to get their food, or will it work for people to get up as they please? Do you want to have volunteers serve the food? The advantage to this is that you can control portions, but the disadvantage is that it is sometimes slower. If people serve themselves, it is much faster to arrange the buffet table so that a line can go along each side of the table.

Timetable of the Evening   Next, plan out the timetable of exactly how the evening will go. Here's a sample timetable for a dinner:

6:00	Guests begin arriving. They mingle, get drinks, and find a place to sit. Volunteers sell last-minute raffle tickets (if a raffle is part of the event).
6:45	Dinner is served.
7:15	Program begins. Emcee welcomes everyone, introduces project very briefly and introduces performance.
7:20	Performance
7:35	Emcee introduces two key members of project. Members describe project, tell personal stories about why they are involved, why issue is important to them.
7:45	Emcee or other speaker introduces honoree, presents award. Honoree speaks about issue and importance of this project.
8:00	A member thanks the honoree, reinforces the importance of the project, makes a strong fundraising pitch, and asks people to put checks in envelopes on their tables.
8:05	Volunteers circulate around the room with baskets to collect contributions.
8:10	Emcee or other speaker holds raffle drawing.
8:25	Emcee closes program, thanks everyone, tells people to stay for dessert.
8:25–9:00	Guests mingle, have dessert, coffee, and tea.

It is important to keep track of time and to keep the program moving; if you are running too late, people will start trickling out before the fundraising pitch, and the event may fizzle instead of ending with a bang. The emcee plays an important role in moving the program along. Let all the speakers and performers know in advance how much time they will have and that someone will be cueing them when they get close to the end of their time. Nevertheless, plan ahead for the inevitable extra time people will take. Have the cue person sit discreetly in the front in easy view of the speaker and hold signs up indicating when the speaker has only a short time left: "3 minutes," "1 minute," "30 seconds," "Stop."

The Pitch   As mentioned earlier, to boost the fundraising from the dinner, ask a persuasive volunteer or member of your project to make a pitch. The person doing the pitch should ask very clearly for a donation, then pause, make sure people have pens and envelopes, and give people enough time to write checks. See the tips on doing the pitch in Resource D.

Step 10: Evaluation and Thank-Yous

Though it might be tempting to run off to the next project, evaluating your event is an important step so you can see if you met the goals you set at the beginning. Here are some questions to ask:

- Did you increase the number of potential volunteers for your project?
- Did you increase your visibility with a targeted constituency or an influential decision maker?
- Are your key leaders who worked on this project excited to work together on other fundraising or nonfundraising projects?
- Are there things that you would change about the dinner planning or logistics if you did this again?

Even if you did not meet your fundraising goals, it is just as important to analyze why. The successes and mistakes you make are important lessons to pass on. Your team should also make a recommendation about whether this event should be repeated—if not, why not, and if so, how. If you decide to do a dinner again, all your records—evaluation records, donor records, workplans, invitation originals, and so on—will make it much easier for people doing an event like this another time and it will probably help them bring in more money next time. So be sure to compile and file these materials. Also, your volunteers have worked hard to put on this dinner, so draw out all the successes and go celebrate.

Thank-yous go a long way toward deepening people's commitment to your project and making them want to return for more and continue being a supporter. Send thank-you notes within a week or two of the event to everyone who attended and all the volunteers who worked on the dinner.

VARIATION ON A DINNER: THE LAOTIAN TRADITIONAL DEDICATION DANCE

According to Torm Nompraseurt of the Laotian Organizing Project and the Asian Pacific Environmental Network in California, a special event that has been quite a hit in the Laotian community is the Laotian traditional dedication dance. The dance is part of a fundraising event and party where people enjoy food and drink and, throughout the night, buy dance rounds in honor of friends, family, and other community members. Torm says that the dance can be used to celebrate the Khmu New Year, an anniversary of an organization, Valentine's Day, or to support the Lao Temple. A live band plays songs that people request—and pay for—from American pop music for the young people to the Lao and Thai songs that the seniors like to swoon to. The key that drives up the fundraising is that the more you pay for your song round, the earlier it gets played, and the more respect it pays to the person you are dedicating it to. Also, if a song is bought and dedicated to you, you usually return the favor and buy a round for that person. A good emcee keeps the crowd excited and the bids flying. Sometimes the dance purchasing can become so frenzied that there is not enough time to play all the songs before the party ends. In that case, the band might play shortened versions of some of the songs to fit all of them in.

In addition to the dance round bidding, the event raises money through admission and by selling flowers, food, and drinks. Like many fundraising strategies, the key to the event is personal relationships. If the organizers of the dance have good relationships with the leader of a clan, the whole clan will come to the dance. Medium-size events have had between two hundred and four hundred people, and dances to celebrate the Lao New Year have seen as many as two thousand attend. The dance is a very important part of the whole event, and it can generate a profit of $2,000 to $4,000.

WOMENADE

A group of women have turned potlucks into pots of gold for homeless residents of Washington, D.C. Dr. Amy Kossoff, a doctor at a homeless clinic, spent thousands of her family's dollars helping her very poor patients buy medicines, eyeglasses, and other necessities. To ease her burden, several of her friends created Womenade. Once or twice a year these women hold a huge potluck dinner. Each woman brings a dish to share and a check for $35. The money goes into an account that Dr. Kossoff uses to help her clients make ends meet. These dinners have become so popular that they now raise thousands of dollars and have been replicated all over the country for many different charitable causes.

LOTERIA

Stephanie's nieces attended a bilingual (Spanish-English) public school in San Francisco called Buena Vista. The students' parents organize an annual fundraising event called "Loteria" that is based on the popular Mexican bingo game of that name. Whole families attend, both for the fun of playing loteria and for the delicious potluck dinner. From a combination of fees charged to play the game and tickets to the dinner itself, this event has raised several hundred dollars each year. While not a huge sum, it is also an opportunity for community building among the families. And because the event is organized by parents and the school donates the space, there are very few expenses.

WORKPLAN

The following workplan provides a summary of the key steps necessary to implement this fundraising strategy and an estimated time frame for each step. It is meant to be a template from which to create your own plan and your own timeline. By taking the time to create a plan and timeline, you'll be more organized, more likely to avoid last-minute crises, and ultimately more successful in raising the money you need.

Workplan 9.1
Community Dinner

What	Who	1	2	3	4	5	6	7	8	9	10	11	12	Done
							When (Week Number)							
1. Make a plan and budget														
Plan overall vision and goals for dinner		x												
Make a budget		x	x											
Make a workplan		x	x											
Decide whether to do additional fundraising activities		x	x											
Identify potential volunteer roles		x	x											
2. Recruit volunteers														
Match volunteers with roles and responsibilities		x	x	x										
Provide training if needed			x	x										
Check in and provide ongoing support				x	x	x	x	x	x	x	x	x	x	
3. Develop invitation list														
Brainstorm invitation list with volunteers and others			x	x										
4. Find a dinner site and set date														
Decide on site needs: child care room, kitchen, size, and so on			x	x										
Call and visit potential sites			x	x										
Finalize site and date					x									
5. Design, print, and send invitations														
Design invitations (logistics, reply card, reply envelope)					x	x								
Print invitations and reply card, buy envelopes						x	x							
Have a mailing party								x						
6. Plan program														
Design program agenda					x	x								
Recruit and prep speakers and performers					x	x	x	x						
Arrange sound system									x	x				
Orchestrate the pitch											x	x		

Workplan 9.1
Community Dinner (continued)

What	Who	When (Week Number) 1	2	3	4	5	6	7	8	9	10	11	12	Done
7. Arrange food, drinks, and other logistics														
Get food and drink donations, decide whether to cook or cater						x	x	x	x					
Buy utensils and other necessary items											x	x		
Decide whether child care is needed and prepare										x	x			
Make a plan for getting into and closing up the dinner site											x	x		
Make any other needed arrangements										x	x	x		
8. Publicize event, do turnout calls, get contributions														
Volunteers sell tickets and get contributions from invitees							x	x	x	x	x	x	x	
Publicize dinner through newspaper, PSAs, flyers									x	x	x	x	x	
Compile and revise registration list										x	x	x	x	
9. Review event details and hold the event														
Do minute-by-minute breakdown and run through with key people												x		
Set up and clean up													x	
Hold the dinner													x	
10. Evaluation and thank-yous														
Evaluate and celebrate with volunteer team													x	
Document event													x	
Send out thank-yous													x	

Bowlathons and Other Pledge-Raising Events

Pledge-raising activities are increasingly common as fundraising and publicity events for a range of causes, the best-known ones being walkathons or bikeathons for health issues such as AIDS, leukemia and lymphoma, and breast cancer. Organized by professional fundraisers or organizations that specialize in producing them, these events require up to a year of advance planning and are relatively complicated to organize. However, you can adapt these events for a smaller organization or project, and they can be organized by a dedicated team of volunteers. This chapter is based on the experience of the Center for Anti-Violence Education in Brooklyn, New York, which had a successful annual bowlathon for many years that was organized almost entirely by volunteers. Applying the organizing principles of other "thons," the bowlathon is ideal for a small group that isn't able to recruit hundreds of people to participate or doesn't need to generate lots of corporate support and sponsorship. While this chapter provides details about doing a bowlathon, it also discusses how you can adapt this material for other pledge events, such as walkathons, swimathons, and bikeathons.

Here is how the bowlathon works. Before the scheduled day of bowling, your volunteer bowling team asks people they know to sponsor them by pledging a contribution either based on the team member's bowling score (an amount per pin) or as a lump sum. Lump sums can be collected before or after the bowling event. A per-pin pledge is collected after the bowling event, at which point the pledge is multiplied by the bowler's score. (An experienced but amateur bowler can expect to get a score of 120 to 140 points, while a total novice might get 80 or 90.) For example, a 20-cent-per-pin pledge multiplied by a score of 90 comes out to a contribution of $18.

Adapted from Lucy Grugett, "The Bowl-a-Thon," *Grassroots Fundraising Journal*, 1993, *12*(1).

Because bowling is an activity that many people have at least some passing experience with, it's easy to get a lot of people in your group to participate in this event. For those who have never bowled, the rudiments are usually picked up easily, and bowling is fun even for the most unskilled player. Kids enjoy it, too.

Other pledge-raising events are organized on the same principle: those participating in the event get contributions from people they know who agree to sponsor them. Come up with pledge events that your volunteers will think is fun. Here are some examples of other pledge events:

- Readathons for kids

- Danceathons (can be a team event with two people or a group effort where the total number of hours someone is dancing is the determining number)

- Individual or small-group bikeathon or walkathon (where total number of miles biked or walked by an individual or small group can be tallied)

- Speechathon (where a group of people speak or debate, or read speeches or writings of famous people, such as Dr. Martin Luther King Jr., the Dalai Lama, or Eleanor Roosevelt, for a certain period of time)

The specific stories at the end of the chapter illustrate other creative pledge events.

BEST USES

Pledge-raising events of all kinds are fun to participate in, and people who might otherwise be reluctant to ask for money find it easier to approach someone to sponsor their participation in an event like this. Sponsors generally find it easy to give to a pledge-raising event because it is usually not a very large contribution, and they can even give a flat donation. Pledge-raising events are a good community-building activity, as people join together to have fun and raise money at the same time. For some people, the physical challenge of a pledge event is a motivating factor in their decision to participate; raising money for a good cause may be secondary.

The bowlathon works well for several reasons. First, it can be carried out by a small group of volunteers. Second, it can be inexpensive to put on. Third, a bowlathon is not dependent on good weather, as are outdoor fundraising events. Fourth, you don't have the complexities of getting permits, disrupting traffic, and dealing with issues of safety that are required for many walks, runs, and bike-riding events.

THINGS TO CONSIDER

You may have no problem recruiting ten of your friends to go bowling, but their willingness to ask people to pledge support for their efforts is what brings in the money.

Because the bowlers are also the folks soliciting contributions, there aren't as many options as with other strategies to divide up the work among many people. So it's important to support and motivate your team of volunteers to make sure they both ask for sponsors *and* collect their contributions before or after the event. Because collecting the money pledged is one of the greatest challenges, people are increasingly asking for the pledges to be paid up front, before the event takes place.

The lead time required for a small-scale pledge event like a bowlathon is about two months. Plan on at least twice that much time for a walkathon, bikeathon, or swimathon that requires finding a location and possibly getting permits.

COSTS

- Rental of bowling lanes
- Photocopying (of solicitation letters, pledge forms, and the like)
- Postage (for soliciting sponsors and sending thank-you notes)
- Refreshments for bowlers
- Prizes for bowlers

MATERIALS NEEDED FOR VOLUNTEERS

- A copy of Resource B, Who Can You Ask?
- Form to track pledge solicitation
- Sample solicitation letter (or preprinted letter with space for handwritten note)
- Response cards
- Envelopes (to mail letter in, plus return envelopes)
- Fact sheet or brief description of project

STEPS TO TAKE

These are the steps you should plan on taking. Each will be discussed in detail.

1. Make a plan

2. Recruit volunteers

3. Secure bowling lanes

4. Conduct a brief training or orientation for volunteers

5. Check in with bowlers on their pledge gathering

6. Hold the bowlathon

7. Follow up to collect pledges

8. Evaluate and send thank-you notes

As you go through the steps in detail, use the sample workplan at the end of the chapter to create a timeline and task list.

Step 1: Make a Plan

Set a date for the bowlathon or other pledge event to take place, making sure you can secure the location (the bowling lanes for bowling, city streets for a walkathon, pool for a swimathon) or get the needed permits. Decide on your fundraising goal, which will tell you how many participants you will need. Assuming that each volunteer walker, bowler, swimmer, or runner can muster $250 from sponsors, you'd need to recruit ten volunteers to reach a fundraising goal of $2,500. Inevitably, people may not be able to collect all of their pledges, so you may want to recruit more participants or make people's pledge goal slightly higher than the actual amount you need them to bring in.

Step 2: Recruit Volunteers

Getting people involved who are willing to bowl (or walk or swim or whatever you have planned) *and* solicit their friends, family, and acquaintances to pledge money for their effort is key to raising money with pledge events. For a bowlathon, it's important to tell potential volunteers that they don't need to have bowled before in order to participate, have fun, and raise money. Use the Volunteer Recruitment Form in Resource A to identify people who might be willing to help out in this and other ways. Here are the things you'll be recruiting people to do:

- Bowl (or walk, swim, bike, run)
- Seek sponsors to support their participation with a donation
- Schedule the event at the bowling lanes
- Draft a sample letter requesting support
- Check in with bowlers on how their pledge-gathering is going
- Help out with logistics on the day of the event
- Follow up with bowlers after the event to collect pledges
- Send thank-you notes to volunteers and donors

Step 3: Secure Appropriate Location

For a bowlathon, keep in mind that many bowling lanes are reserved by leagues, so make reservations a couple of months in advance. If you don't have that much lead time, you can still inquire at your local bowling lanes about possible available times for a group event. Ask if the lanes might donate the cost of games as a contribution. Usually, they will at least throw in the shoe rental. In the San Francisco Bay Area, games cost about $4.00 each and shoe rentals cost $4.25. If the lanes won't donate the games or the shoes, you can ask the volunteers to pay for the cost of playing.

When making reservations, plan on about four people per lane. Two games with four people per lane take between an hour and a half and two hours.

For some pledge events, such as walkathons and swimathons, the location where the event is held may require you to obtain liability insurance to cover anyone who is injured in the course of the activity.

Step 4: Conduct a Brief Training or Orientation for Volunteers

Bring people together to talk about the process of soliciting pledges, how to make a good pitch, and what the overall goals of the bowlathon are. At this gathering, circulate pledge forms and "how-to" instructions. (See Chapter Five for detailed examples of how to conduct a training with volunteers to increase their comfort and confidence with asking for money—or, in this case, for pledges of sponsorship.)

Allow three to four weeks for people to collect pledges before the event. With more time, momentum is lost; less time has the obvious drawback of not allowing people to reach as many potential sponsors as possible.

Pledge sheets, such as Worksheet 10.1, should keep track of the contributors' names, the amounts pledged per pin (or lump-sum amount), and the total collected. Ask bowlers to collect contributors' addresses and phone numbers when they sign them up so that you can send them a thank-you note (and if this is part of an ongoing project or organization, so you can add them to your mailing list for future solicitations). In the constant struggle to find new supporters, this can be an effective way to expand your donor base.

Instructions to the volunteers, as in Exhibit 10.1, should explain the rudiments of the bowlathon and outline the per-point and lump-sum pledge options. Include a couple of sample pitches, including why your project or organization is so important and what sponsors' contributions will pay for. Also include in the instructions the date of the event, the bowling lanes' address and phone number, the cost of participating (if bowlers must pay for games or shoes), and the names and phone numbers of the event's organizers.

The following sample letter to potential sponsors gives volunteers an idea of how to approach people.

Dear Friends,

I'm about to do something I've never done before—and I'm hoping you can help! On December 5 (just six weeks from now), I'm going to go bowling. Well, what's so impressive about that, you ask?

This is not just any bowling experience. Not only have I never set foot in a bowling alley, but I'm doing it to raise money for an organization that is near and dear to my heart and is trying to get an important project off the ground.

You may know that since our current governor was elected two years ago, the state budget allocations for much-needed community health clinics (which serve 80 percent of the rural population of our state) has been cut by more than 30 percent. At our local clinic, this has meant that we haven't been able to develop any prevention programs for the increasing numbers of teens who have been using our services.

Recently, the teen members of the clinic's advisory council proposed the establishment of a peer counseling program that will help the teenage patients of the clinic deal with issues of teen sexuality, including sexually transmitted diseases, birth control, and sexual orientation. They feel that some teenagers don't feel comfortable discussing these issues with the adult staff members of the clinic, but that there is a lot of information and support they desperately need.

Because all of us on the advisory council feel this project is an exciting and important new program initiative, and one that will be relatively inexpensive to run (the peer counselors will all be volunteers), we're working hard to find sources of funding. That's why I'm approaching you and other people like you—members of the community who care about the health of our young people.

So, on December 5, I will join about twenty-five other people, including ten teens, as we bowl for dollars! I'm writing to ask if you would be willing to sponsor me in this historic display of my bowling prowess. I'm hoping you'll consider a contribution of $25 to $50, but any support you can give would be greatly appreciated.

I'll call you soon to follow up on this letter and answer any questions you may have. Thanks for considering my request.

Sincerely,

Bessie Long

Keep the tips in Handout 10.1 in mind as you make your calls following up on your letters.

Step 5: Check in with Bowlers on Their Pledge Gathering

This is the key, of course, to a successful event, and it is the organizer's main task. Depending on how often you're in regular contact with the volunteers anyway (such as in weekly or monthly meetings, daily classes, and so on) this will vary, but momentum must build to the day of the event. If you have an office that volunteers or members are likely to visit regularly, consider having have a sign-up poster at the office where bowlers add their names and the number of sponsors they have. If you have a Web site, create a page that is updated regularly with the number of sponsors solicited and amount of money raised to date. You can also use phone

Worksheet 10.1
Pledge Form

Use this form to keep track of the people you solicit for sponsorships. Write down their name and contact information, and note the date that you complete each step in the process.

My score: _____

Sponsor's name and contact info (include phone and e-mail)	Date solicited (by letter, phone, or e-mail)	Date of follow-up and result	Amount pledged (lump sum or per pin)	Pledge collected (date and amount)
Cecilia Ortiz 1122 Oak St. (323) 555-4444 cortiz@igc.org	5/25—sent e-mail	6/5—Called, l.m. 6/8—Called, yes!	Pledged $35	6/30—rec'd. check for $35

Exhibit 10.1
Sample Instructions to Bowlers

Thank you for agreeing to participate in the bowlathon for health, a fundraiser for our local community health center. Your efforts will help us raise much-needed funds to start a peer counseling program for teens on issues of sexuality and reproductive health.

Here's what we're asking you to do:

1. Using the attached pledge form, solicit people you know to sponsor you in the upcoming bowlathon. They can either pledge a specific amount ($15, $25, $100, for example) or an amount based on your bowling score. For example, if your score for one game is 95 and your friend wants to sponsor you at 25 cents per pin, they will pay you $23.75. While a specific amount is easier for everyone (you can collect the money at the time you're asking for their pledge, saving you time and effort after the bowlathon is over, and you'll know how much you've raised), some people find it more fun and a greater challenge to base their money raised on their bowling score. If you're planning to send a letter requesting support and then follow up with your potential pledgers by phone, use the sample letter in this packet as a guide to writing your own letter, or just use it as is.

2. Send in your pledge form with whatever money you've collected in advance to the office, Attention: Susana Gomez, by no later than Friday, November 28. Keep a copy of the pledge form so you know who to follow up with after the bowlathon is over.

3. Arrive at the bowling alley at noon, ready to play! You will be matched up with three other bowlers to play with. If you already have a group that wants to bowl together, please let Susana know in advance.

4. Follow up with your pledgers the week after the bowlathon, and send in any money you collect.

Essential Information:

Date and time of bowlathon: Saturday, December 5, 2:00–5:00 P.M.

Location: Community Lanes, 2500 Main Street

Have questions or need more information? Call or e-mail Susana Gomez, 555-5555, susana@communityhealth.org.

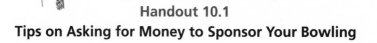

Handout 10.1
Tips on Asking for Money to Sponsor Your Bowling

- Talk about what the cause means to you and your personal connection to the issue.

- Remember that people like to give money to people and causes they care about.

- Practice first with a friend.

- Be open to any questions your potential supporters may have and take an interest in what they care about (in relation to your cause).

- Don't worry about being able to answer every question a prospect may have. You can always tell them that you'll find out from someone who knows more about it.

- After you ask, stop talking! Wait for them to respond. They may respond with a question or say they have to think about it, but don't assume you know what they're going to say.

- If they say yes, make a plan for how you're going to collect their payment.

- Always thank your prospects whether they give or not (for taking the time to think about it, for giving, for supporting you in whatever way they can).

trees and e-mail to urge people on. The biggest motivator, however, is that volunteers believe in the organization and want to help raise money to support it.

Step 6: Hold the Bowlathon

One or two organizers are needed for the day's event, depending on the size of the group. Confirm your reservation with the bowling venue the week before. As bowlers arrive, assign them to lanes; when a lane has the required number of bowlers, they can begin to play. The organizer can collect bowling fees from everyone, or she can assign a lane leader to take charge of each group. During the outing or at the end, you can give out inexpensive, funny prizes to add to the group's pleasure and also as an excuse to bring folks together, thank them for coming out, and exhort them to go out and collect their pledges. Entertaining categories have included most original form, most enthusiastic bowler, best dressed, and the more mundane highest and lowest scorer.

Step 7: Follow Up with Pledgers and Collect Money

Keep momentum going after the bowling day as bowlers go back to their sponsors to collect the pledges. Sponsors will probably want to know their bowler's score or the total results of the "thon," so play this up! Remind people with e-mails and phone calls encouraging them to follow up with their pledgers as soon after the event as possible. Otherwise, momentum will be lost—and so will some of the money pledged.

Step 8: Send Thank-You Notes

After pledges have been collected, ask bowlers to send thank-you notes to their supporters. If you plan to do future fundraising activities, let the contributors know that you will keep them informed of the progress of your work and will include them on your mailing list. Many who first give through a pledge event will continue to support your work from one year to the next.

Send those who participated in the event a thank-you note as well, thanking them for the specific amount they raised, giving the overall score or result, and telling them how much money was raised because of their efforts.

CLEANATHON

Nokomis Healthy Seniors Program, based in Minneapolis, helps seniors continue living independently in their homes. Board members organized a "cleanathon" in which they recruited volunteers to spend a Saturday morning cleaning the homes of some of the seniors the group serves. The volunteers went in teams and tackled cleaning projects that were difficult for the seniors to do themselves, such as washing windows and scrubbing floors. Before the day of the cleanathon, volunteers asked friends and acquaintances to sponsor them in their volunteer cleaning effort by giving a financial contribution to the organization. The first year of the cleanathon, with virtually no staff involvement, the volunteers raised $2,000. The second year, with a little experience under their belts, they raised more than $4,000, made possible partly by a matching gift from a local corporation.

PROTESTATHON

A creative use of the pledge event has been employed to raise money for pro-lesbian, gay, bisexual, transgender causes. It was inspired as a way to challenge Fred Phelps, the infamous antigay pastor of the Westboro Baptist Church in Topeka, Kansas, who organizes pickets around the country to assert that God hates gay people. Phelps's group uses outrageous tactics, such as protesting at the funerals of gay people. He hit the national spotlight when his group protested the funeral of Matthew Sheperd, the twenty-one-year-old gay man brutally killed in Wyoming in 1998.

An Ann Arbor businessman, Keith Orr, co-owner of the Aütbar, has been credited with coming up with a way to use Phelps's antics to raise money for gay causes. He urged people to make pledges based on the length of time the Westboro protestors stayed outside his business in 2001. "We had some pledge a dollar a minute, and others pledge only a nickel a minute, but it all added up," he said. In his first attempt, he made $8,000 for a local gay-rights organization. In Huntington, West Virginia, in a similar response to a Phelps local protest, groups or individuals pledged donations for each minute of Phelps's rally or for each time his protesters said selected words. Flat-fee pledges were also accepted. The money collected went to the local human relations commission to support diversity education.

In conjunction with the fundraiser, a local coalition of groups hosted a speak-out against Phelps, and the Huntington High School Gay-Straight Alliance scheduled a rally and dance.

WORKPLAN

The following workplan provides a summary of the key steps necessary to implement this fundraising strategy and an estimated time frame for each step. It is meant to be a template from which to create your own plan and your own timeline. By taking the time to create a plan and timeline, you'll be more organized, more likely to avoid last-minute crises, and ultimately more successful in raising the money you need.

Workplan 10.1
Bowlathon

What	Who	When (Week Number)										Done
		1	2	3	4	5	6	7	8	9	10	
1. Make a plan		x										
2. Recruit volunteers			x									
3. Set date and secure bowling lanes			x									
4. Conduct brief training or orientation for volunteers				x								
5. Check in with bowlers on pledge gathering						x	x	x	x			
6. Hold the bowlathon									x			
7. Follow up to collect pledges										x	x	
8. Evaluate and send thank-yous											x	

Auctions

Auctions, whether of the live, silent, or more recently, online variety, are a popular and versatile method of fundraising. They can be the entire focus of a fundraising event or an add-on to a dinner, cultural event, or other gathering of your supporters.

There are two major kinds of auctions: live auctions with a skilled auctioneer, and silent auctions, where people write their bids next to displayed items.

Depending on the goods or services being auctioned, auctions can raise from several hundred to several thousand dollars. This chapter describes how to do a relatively simple live or silent auction that should raise between $500 and $5,000.

BEST USES

Auctions can be a lot of fun, both for those organizing and for the people attending.

Silent auctions are great add-ons to a special event, and it's possible to do a silent auction on a scale small enough to keep it manageable and still raise money. At a community potluck, for example, auctioning off ten to twenty low-budget items could add $250 to $1,000 to your event's income.

The key to a successful auction is the combination of donations of high-quality goods and services that people may want and a large enough group of people interested in bidding on them.

THINGS TO CONSIDER

Like all special events, auctions are labor-intensive to organize and therefore require a core of dedicated volunteers. Without a team of volunteers, too much work will fall on the shoulders of too few people and will result in too little money raised for the amount of time and effort spent.

There are a large number of details to keep track of in planning and running an auction, so this is an event for people who are extremely attentive to details.

Auctions need enough people to attend and participate in bidding. According to auctioneer Sandy Bradley, author of *Benefit Auctions: A Fresh Formula for Grassroots Fundraising,* you need critical mass for a "real-time" auction to be financially successful. She suggests there be a minimum of twenty-five people in the bidding audience and at least two people for every item you're auctioning. In other words, an auction with fifteen items to be bid on needs a bidding audience of at least thirty people.

A live auction will rise and fall on the personality of the auctioneer. While it would be ideal to have a professional auctioneer rattling off numbers and encouraging the crowd, a volunteer who is fast talking and able to hold the attention of the audience might do just as well. The energy of a live auction is created in large part by a number of people bidding against each other. If a lot of your audience doesn't bid on the items, your auction can seem flat. Therefore, if your group is new to putting on an auction, we recommend starting with a silent auction your first time out. It's also possible to do a combination of a silent and live auction in one of two ways: have most of the items bid on silently, but have a few choice ones auctioned off live; or have all the items bid on silently, then an auctioneer visits each item and solicits bids to exceed those on the bid sheet (this way you're starting from a higher base bid).

COSTS

The following items should be considered as potential costs when producing an auction. You should, of course, try to get as many as possible donated.

- Space
- Equipment
- Tables and chairs
- Insurance
- Auctioneer's fee
- Invitation design, printing, and postage
- Publicity (flyers, ads)
- Catalogue design and printing

- Materials for displaying silent auction items
- Decorations
- Food and drink
- Paper goods
- Postage for thank-you letters

As you go through the steps in detail, use the sample workplan at the end of the chapter to create a timeline and task list.

STEPS TO TAKE

These are the steps you should plan on taking. Each will be discussed in detail.

1. Make a plan
2. Recruit volunteers
3. Prepare volunteers to solicit items
4. Solicit items to be auctioned
5. Plan program and logistics of event
6. Publicize the auction
7. Make follow-up calls to invitees
8. Make final preparations
9. Hold the auction
10. Send thank-yous and evaluate

Step 1: Make a Plan

Decide whether to do a live or silent auction, or a combination of the two. In either case, you'll need to decide what kind of event to hold—a simple gathering where the auction is the main feature, or a larger party, dinner, or cultural event of which the auction is a part. That decision will be based on how much money you want to raise and how many people you can count on to help carry out the event. You will also need to choose a date for the event and create a timeline detailing what has to be done, with deadlines.

Once you know how much money you want to raise, plan to obtain donations of goods and services that are worth twice that amount. This way you will be able to meet your goal even if bids amount to only 50 percent of the value of each item. For example, if you want the auction to raise $5,000, you will need to have items worth a total of $10,000 to be auctioned. Moreover, because about half the people you ask to donate items will decline, you will actually need to plan to solicit $20,000 worth of items.

Step 2: Recruit Volunteers

Use Resource A, Volunteer Recruitment Form, to help you identify people you might recruit to help out with the auction. Here are some of the things you'll want to ask people to do:

- Solicit items to be auctioned

- Organize logistics of the event

- Help publicize the event

- Get lists of people and organizations to send—and e-mail—publicity about the auction

- Help out at the event itself

Step 3: Prepare Volunteers to Solicit Items

Before sending volunteers out to solicit items for the auction, bring them together to brainstorm whom to ask and to conduct an orientation to the process of asking. You'll want to come up with a master list of who is being solicited in order to avoid having one person inadvertently asked by two different solicitors.

It's helpful if the auction items are grouped by category, such as vacations, services, electronics, household goods, or restaurants. Make a list of all the vendors who might donate something and what you want to ask them for, such as dinner for two, a weekend getaway at a vacation cabin, and so on. Remember that people who own small businesses, particularly storefronts, get asked for donations frequently. They might turn you down for a number of reasons not having to do with your group—they may have policies against making donations, they may have donated to five other charities and are not giving to any more at the moment, or it may be a hard time for their business. Therefore, it's good to have at least two and preferably three times as many potential sources of donations as you ultimately need. Handout 11.1 lists some ideas for items to solicit.

Step 4: Solicit Items to Be Auctioned

In this step, volunteers solicit the items for the auction. This may take a couple of steps: a letter requesting an item with a promise to follow up in a few days, then a visit. In cases where the volunteer knows the prospect, they can just make a phone call and follow up with a letter of confirmation if the person agrees to donate something. In other cases, they might want to send a short letter first, stating what they'd like the person to donate and what cause or organization the auction is supporting.

Give this step plenty of time—two months is ideal. People need that time to send out donation letters, make follow-up calls, track people down to get their commitments to donate items, and then actually obtain the items.

Solicitors can help merchants think about how giving an item to your organization is good for their business. Selling points to the merchant include the number of people expected to attend the auction who will see the merchant's name listed with the item, other publicity you are going to do, a promise not to ask for another item this year, or whatever is true for your group. You will likely have greater success getting items donated by merchants you know personally, or whom your organization does business with, or who you know believe in the cause you're raising money for. Start with them. Here's a sample letter asking for a donation to your auction:

> Dear Friend (or Merchant),
>
> I'm writing to ask you to help support a newly formed artists cooperative, Art for All Abilities (AAA). This nonprofit group highlights the work of artists with disabilities in our community. We're planning the first of what we hope will be an annual event: a community potluck and silent auction. I'm hoping you will donate a gift certificate of $25 (or more) to your store to be auctioned off at this event.
>
> The purpose of AAA is to break the isolation that many people with disabilities experience in our community by bringing disabled artists together in exhibition and in creating communal art projects.

We are an all-volunteer project and need to raise money to pay for the expenses of producing exhibits and other programs. This year, we're trying to raise $10,000. Your support of the upcoming silent auction will help us to reach that goal.

We're expecting at least one hundred people to attend the auction and more than one thousand others will hear about the event and the generosity of donors like you through our Web site and upcoming newsletter.

Enclosed is a donation form for you to fill out and return to us if you can contribute a gift certificate (or other item) to this fundraising effort. We greatly appreciate whatever you can give.

I will be calling to follow up within the next couple of weeks and to answer any questions you may have.

Sincerely,

(Name of Volunteer)

Exhibit 11.1 shows a sample form to include with the letter. Merchants should be asked to fill it out and return it so you can keep track of what's being donated and get any instructions about how the gift should be handled.

During the time that volunteers are soliciting donated items, check in with them regularly to see how they're doing and what kind of support they need if they're having a hard time completing their solicitations. Be prepared to help people with problem solving and to provide encouragement to keep the momentum going.

Worksheet 11.1 can help in tracking progress on getting auction items.

Step 5: Plan Program and Logistics of the Event

Once the process of soliciting items for the auction is under way, you can start paying more attention to the details required to hold a successful event. First, decide whether you want to have speakers or entertainment in addition to the auction itself. If so, consider whether people will sit or stand during that part of the event and figure that into your site selection. Second, find a venue for the auction that is large enough to accommodate the number of people you expect for the program you envision, has enough well-lit space to display all of the silent auction items, or, for a live auction, has a stage or elevated platform. In addition, you'll need a place to store the donated items ahead of time.

Goods and Services to Solicit for Your Auction

When thinking about auction items to solicit, remember to ask your team of volunteers what *they* can offer, as well as who they know who might be able to contribute something. Think, too, about whom your organization does business with and whether they might be a potential source of an auction item. Here are some ideas.

Gift certificates from local retailers:

- Bookstores
- Sporting goods stores
- Clothing stores
- Restaurants
- Movie theaters

Services:

- Massages
- Haircuts
- Home-cooked dinners
- Babysitting

Vacations:

- Airline tickets
- Frequent flyer miles
- Night at a bed and breakfast

Classes or personalized instruction:

- Foreign-language instruction
- Music lessons
- Knitting, sewing, gardening
- Self-defense
- Yoga, tai chi, or the like

Things people like:

- DVD player
- Television
- Electronic organizer
- Basket of skin care products or small food items
- Home-baked cakes, cookies, pies

Exhibit 11.1
Auction Donor Form

Art for All Abilities (AAA)
Annual Auction—Donor Form

Thank you for your contribution to AAA's silent auction, taking place on June 25. Please complete this form and return it to our office no later than May 18.

DONATION: Please describe each donation in detail for display and catalogue purposes—for example, "Two $50 gift certificates," "A one-hour Swedish massage," "Frequent-flyer miles for one ticket anywhere in the United States." If possible, please include a brochure, photograph, or information sheet. Be sure to specify location, if applicable, and any limitations, such as availability or excluded items.

_____

_____

_____

☐ Items or gift certificates included

☐ Please make up a gift certificate for me

☐ I will send or deliver my donation by May 18

☐ Please send a volunteer to pick up my donation

Offer expiration date: _____   Retail value: $_____

Minimum bid: $_____

IMPORTANT! The donor will be acknowledged in auction displays and catalogue. To remain anonymous, please check here: _____

_____ Business donor _____ Individual donor

Donor Name _____

Contact Name *(if business donor)* _____

Mailing Address _____

City, State, ZIP _____   E-Mail _____

Day Phone _____   Evening Phone _____

Donor Signature _____   Date _____

Please return form by May 18 to AAA, Box 124, St. Louis, MO 63166.
_____

Adapted from NARAL ProChoice Oregon.

Worksheet 11.1
Auction Items Tracking Form

Name and contact info	Type of item	Date letter sent	Date of follow-up (call or in-person)	Result	Next steps, comments
Rosie's Restaurant 1122 First St. Yourtown	Dinner for two	5/20	June 1—l.m. June 5—talked to Rosie	Yes to gift certificate for $50	Rosie will send in form w/gift certificate.
Gerry's Gems	Gift certificate	5/25	6/8	Can't this year	Said OK to try again next year

Step 6: Publicize the Auction

This step has four parts:

Send invitations by mail. Create an invitation and a reply card and envelope to make it easy for people to respond and to send in a contribution if they can't attend the event. In addition, you may want to create a flyer that you can mail to organizations for posting and that they can photocopy and distribute to other people. Send invitations or flyers to everyone on your mailing list as well as to people whom members of your auction team know but who may not know your organization yet. If you already have some auction items donated, including a list of sample items that will be auctioned off may entice people to come. If you have a lot of lead time, you can even put together a catalogue with pictures or at least descriptions of the majority of the auction items. If you collect items after the catalogue gets printed and goes out, you can distribute an addendum on the day of the auction.

Send invitations virtually. Send an e-mail message to anyone you have an e-mail address for announcing the event. Use or attach the flyer to give your announcement sparkle, and provide an easy way for them to e-mail back their reply (or provide a link to your Web site).

Use your Web site. If your organization has a Web site, post information and the flyer about the auction there, with examples of items that are being auctioned and all the details visitors need in order to attend. Include a reply button.

Use whatever other free publicity outlets you can think of. Some options may include ads in community papers, public service announcements on your local radio stations, and announcements in your sister organizations' e-newsletters.

Step 7: Make Follow-Up Calls to Invitees

The success of an auction—that is, how much money you raise—depends on how many people attend and engage in the bidding. Ask your volunteers to follow up on the invitations they sent to people they know by calling these people about two weeks before the auction is scheduled to take place. A reminder call like this can make the difference between someone showing up to the event or completely forgetting about it. Consider getting your volunteers together for two evenings during which everyone calls their own lists along with anyone else who received an invitation.

Step 8: Make Final Preparations

For live and silent auctions, the details of organizing the event itself are similar to those for any entertainment or program, including setting up the space to allow for the best presentation of items and traffic flow so people can easily place bids, preparing or purchasing food or working with a caterer, and so on.

For a live auction, you will need to create a catalogue that contains a description of each item and the minimum bid for that item. A catalogue can be as simple as a text-only list printed from a computer onto a plain sheet of paper (or several sheets) or as sophisticated as a small, bound booklet with photographs of each item next to the descriptions. Start putting this together as soon as the auction items start coming in and at least a couple of weeks before the auction in order to give yourself plenty of time to get any missing information on the items and to design and print the catalogue. If you have enough people involved, you can expand the catalogue to include ads from some of the donating merchants or others, which will bring in additional income. Print enough copies so that everyone can receive one as they arrive and look through it during the social time before the auction begins. Decide in what order you will auction off (or display) the items. Usually you start with lower-priced items that you think a number of people will want to bid on, then move to more expensive items as people get warmed up and more excited about the bidding.

For a silent auction, prepare a form to place in front of each item that has a description of the item, the name of the donor (if not anonymous), and indicates the minimum bid and in what increments additional bids can be placed. For example, a gift basket of skin-care products that would sell at your local bath store for $30 might have a minimum bid of $20, with increments of $5. A trip to Hawaii, flight and accommodations included, worth $2,000, might have a minimum bid of $1,000, with bidding increments of $100. See Exhibit 11.2 for a sample bidding sheet for a silent auction.

Finally, assign volunteers to the various activities that need to be carried out during the auction, as detailed in Exhibit 11.3.

Step 9: Hold the Auction

It's a good idea to create and distribute "auction rules" to everyone as they arrive at the auction. Exhibit 11.4 presents a sample you can use.

```
┌─────────────────────────────────────────────────────────────────┐
│                                                                   │
│                           Exhibit 11.2                            │
│                 Sample Bid Sheet for Silent Auction               │
│  ───────────────────────────────────────────────────────────     │
│                                                                   │
│  Item 15 (This corresponds to the number in the catalogue.)       │
│  Item: One-hour Swedish massage by Sophia Walker                  │
│  Value: $75                                                       │
│                                                                   │
│  Minimum bid: $50                                                 │
│  Minimum additional bid: $5                                       │
│                                                                   │
│  Name of bidder                    Amount of bid                  │
│                                                                   │
│  _____        $_____         │
│                                                                   │
│  _____        $_____         │
│                                                                   │
│  _____        $_____         │
│                                                                   │
│  _____        $_____         │
│                                                                   │
│  _____        $_____         │
│                                                                   │
│  _____        $_____         │
│                                                                   │
└─────────────────────────────────────────────────────────────────┘
```

For a live auction, it's important that the people attending are serious about bidding. Otherwise, you risk both not selling enough to raise the money you had planned for and not having the excitement of bidding to make the event an enjoyable one for the guests. One way to ensure that the bidders will be enthusiastic is to assess the donated items to make sure they will be of interest to bidders. If you feel something is worth much more than people attending the auction will be willing to spend on it, make arrangements to sell it outside of the auction. For example, at a neighborhood association's auction for which residents donated many wonderful items, an antique broach was offered that the auction organizers had valued by an antique dealer. While the broach was certainly worth its $250 appraised value, it was too old fashioned for the audience's taste. To save the feelings of the elderly neighborhood resident who donated the item, the organization sold it to an antique jewelry dealer for more money than they thought it would bring at the auction.

Check-In Table Attendants

Both tables can hand out programs or catalogues.

Table 1 (pay as you enter): These volunteers collect money for entrance fee (if there is one) and have all auction attendants who receive bidding paddles sign a form of agreement to pay for any item on which they place the winning bid.

Table 2 (express service): These volunteers check in people who have paid in advance to attend the event; they may have already signed the agreement form and received their bidding paddle in the mail. Have extra forms and paddles available in case people forget to bring them.

Greeters and Ushers

These volunteers will be able to answer guest questions, such as where to find restrooms and what time events begin and end. They can also serve as floaters between tables and other volunteer stations and help out wherever needed.

Silent Auction Table Closers

These volunteers are responsible for circling the winning bids on the silent auction sheets (which should be in duplicate) and giving them to the cashier; they can also be responsible for moving items from tables to the checkout area.

Recorder

This volunteer keeps track of winning bids and the number of the winning bidder, filling out sheets in duplicate or triplicate: one sheet stays with the recorder; the other two go to the cashier. When a person is checking out, they receive one copy as their receipt. These receipts record the auction item and item number as listed in the catalogue, the winning bidder's number, and the amount the item sold for.

Runners

These volunteers run the receipt from the recorder to the check-out table or cashier.

Spotters

These volunteers help the auctioneer spot people in the audience who are trying to bid, but whom the auctioneer may not otherwise see.

Paperwork and Checkout Attendants

Several people should be doing this job. Depending on how many people are attending the auction, you may want to break up the checkout and cashier lines into sections (for example, bidder numbers 1 to 25 in one line, 26 to 50 in the next, and so forth). The cashier station should keep a file box (or several, depending on how many bidders there are) containing separate folders for each bidder. These folders should contain all the receipts for items that have been sold, as well as the agreement form signed at the beginning of the evening. When a bidder checks out, they will turn in their bid paddle, and the cashier will open their folder to find the receipts for the items the bidder won and collect payment. Most of the goods should be in the cashier area so the cashier or a helper will be able to turn over the goods at this point. Items that are too large to carry may require special delivery or pickup arrangements.

As part of the preparations for the auction, think through how people will pay for and collect the items they've acquired. You want to avoid having a pile-up of people coming to pay for their items at the end of the evening, which makes an otherwise enjoyable experience irritating. So have several volunteers ready to collect money and distribute the items, as well as enough space set aside for that task. In addition, make arrangements for winners who have to leave early to be able to claim and pay for their items without disturbing the ongoing auction. If at all possible, arrange to be able to accept credit card payments for the items people have bought. This option is especially important if you have any high-ticket items, such as expensive art work or vacations. As people pay for their treasures, remind them that these are not tax-deductible donations.

Exhibit 11.4
Auction Rules

Silent Auction Rules

When you arrive, we will give you a bidding number. All items on the silent auction table have an adjacent bid sheet. Enter your bid legibly, writing your bid number opposite the desired bid amount. We will announce each closing, at which time all bidding on that section ceases. The closing bid circled by an auction official constitutes the winning bid. If you are the highest bidder, you enter into a legal contract to buy (as per the agreement signed upon entrance to the auction).

Live Auction Rules

To bid on an item, raise your bid card so that the auctioneer can acknowledge it. You are the successful bidder when the auctioneer says "Sold" and acknowledges your bid number. If you are the highest bidder, you enter into a legal contract to buy. In the event of a dispute between bidders, the auctioneer shall have sole discretion to determine the winning bid.

General Auction Policies

- All sales are final. No refunds or returns.
- All items are sold "as is" and must be removed at the end of the evening. Payments may be made by check, cash, or credit card.
- A paid "receipt" is required to remove an item.
- The organization and its successors, as well as the auctioneer, have endeavored to describe and catalogue the items correctly, but all items are sold "as is" and the organization and the auctioneer neither warrants nor represents, and shall in no event be held responsible for, the correctness of description, genuineness, authorship, provenance or condition of an item. No statement contained in the catalogue or made orally at the sale or elsewhere shall be deemed to be such a warranty, representation or assumption of liability.
- The organization reserves the right to withdraw any item prior to the call for bids. A minimum bid has been established on all items. The organization shall have the right to reject any bid at any time prior to the item being sold and to reject any advance not deemed sufficient.

Step 10: Send Thank-Yous and Evaluate

Send thank-you notes to everyone who attended the auction as well as to each person who sold tickets and each merchant and others who donated items.

If you think you might want to conduct another auction in the future, evaluation is crucial to making improvements and potentially raising more money the next time. Your evaluation can be a simple set of notes jotted down (legibly) soon after the auction is over, perhaps at a final wrap-up meeting of the auction team. Note how many items were sold, which were the most popular, any problems with the volunteers, the merchants, the logistics, and so on. Make a file with all the information about the auction, including lists of who donated items, who purchased items, volunteers, and notes about timing and other issues. The following year, it will be much simpler to do the auction if a committee can pull out the file and benefit from the previous year's experience.

VARIATION ON A THEME: THE ONLINE AUCTION

If you don't have the resources to organize an event—involving finding a space, providing refreshments, getting people to attend, and all the other details of an in-person auction—an online auction may be a great alternative. Online auctions take place virtually. People go to a Web site, view the items to bid on, and submit their bid. Anyone familiar with Web sites like eBay will understand the process of placing bids online. Online auctions work well with a community of people who are comfortable with and have easy access to the Internet. They also lend themselves to a geographically dispersed community, because they don't require people to go anywhere in order to participate. Keep in mind that the donated items must be easily sent to the winners; moreover, some items won't work for people outside of your community. For example, a dinner for two in Chicago won't get many bids from your supporters in Houston. Online auctions don't require those bidding to have a high level of commitment to the cause, so long as the items you are auctioning off are appealing to the audience you expect to bid on them and you have a way of publicizing the event and its Web site widely.

Online auctions are not the best strategy if you're trying to build a sense of community, if you want to celebrate something with a group of people, or even if you want to increase people's understanding of the issue you're raising money for. However, they are a way to get people who are more peripheral to your organization bringing money into the organization for something they want that also supports a good cause.

Online auctions do have some costs, some of which you may be able to get donated:

- Web designer to create the site

- Fees for the domain to host the site

- Printing and postage to send letters to people soliciting items to auction

- Postage to ship items to winners (amount will vary depending on the items; if most of them are gift certificates, cost will be minimal)

- Printing and mailing flyers to advertise the auction

You will need plenty of lead time to create the Web site and post the items to be auctioned off. If you are using a volunteer Web designer, build in extra time. Take digital photographs of any physical items that will be auctioned so that the image can be posted. For tickets, gift certificates, and so on, create a generic image that you can use. Decide on a minimum bid for each item as well as the increments for increasing a bid.

Of course, being sure the technology is working is the most important issue. Before the official launch of the auction, be sure all items have been posted on the Web site and that the mechanism for submitting bids is working smoothly. When someone posts a bid, it should show up immediately so it's clear in what order identical bids came in and so that those bidding know the most recent bid.

As the auction gets under way, monitor the level of bidding activity to determine if you need to increase publicity to get more people involved. Once the auction is closed, make sure winners have paid for their items before they receive them. The easiest system is to have them mail in a check, at which point their item is mailed. If you have the capability of accepting credit card payments, or using an online payment service such as PayPal, then purchasers can pay online.

WORKPLAN

The following workplan provides a summary of the key steps necessary to implement this fundraising strategy and an estimated time frame for each step. It is meant to be a template from which to create your own plan and your own timeline. By taking the time to create a plan and timeline, you'll be more organized, more likely to avoid last-minute crises, and ultimately more successful in raising the money you need.

Workplan 11.1
Auction

What	Who	1	2	3	4	5	6	7	8	9	10	11	Done
1. Make a plan													
Make a budget		x											
Decide on live or silent auction (or both)		x											
Identify potential volunteer roles		x											
2. Recruit volunteers			x	x									
3. Prepare volunteers to solicit items				x	x								
4. Solicit auction items				x	x	x	x	x					
Make follow-up calls to volunteer solicitors					x	x	x	x	x				
5. Plan program and logistics													
Find a location			x	x									
Find an auctioneer (live auction only)				x	x								
Line up entertainment or speakers					x	x	x						
Make food and drink arrangements					x	x	x						
6. Publicize													
Design, print, and mail invitations					x	x	x						
Prepare other publicity (flyers, ads, e-mail)							x	x					
7. Make follow-up calls to invitees										x			
8. Make final preparations													
Prepare auction catalogue								x	x	x			
Set up for event										x	x		
Finalize the details: food, drink, people to help out									x	x	x		
9. Hold the auction											x		
10. Send thank-yous and evaluate												x	

When (Week Number)

Selling

Ad Books

An ad book project raises money from local businesses, corporations, and other people you know by selling them advertising space in a program, auction catalogue, resource directory, or other printed item. These books are usually produced in conjunction with an event, but they can be used in other ways as well. Ad books can be as simple as a couple of folded sheets of paper with ads printed on both sides or as complicated as a program book with color advertisements.

BEST USES

An ad book is an ideal strategy to use with events such as a community dinner, a concert, sports event, or political event where there might already be a printed program and an audience to distribute the ad book to. Ad books can also be easily attached to real resources that already have some distribution method, such as a directory or resource handbook. For example, a consumer health care rights organization publishes a "know your rights" handbook for its members and other health care consumers that informs people about state and federal laws that protect consumers and contains contact information for health care providers, health care advocates, and organizing groups. The group distributes the handbook by giving them directly to their members and leaving them in clinic waiting rooms. Throughout the handbook appear advertisements from ally organizations, small businesses, and health care providers. The most lucrative advertisers are the larger health care providers and insurance companies that have large advertising budgets and place ads in order to appear to be good community partners.

Ad books are a good way to get support from small businesses or people who may not otherwise give you a contribution but who have an advertising budget. These

Parts of this chapter were adapted from Kim Klein, *Fundraising for Social Change,* 4th ed. (San Francisco: Jossey-Bass, 2000).

183

advertisers may want to reach the people your ad book will be distributed to. Advertisers know that many people like to patronize businesses that are supportive of the community, and taking out an ad is a public way of demonstrating their support.

Members and volunteers of your project who are more reluctant to ask for direct contributions may find it easier to sell ads to small businesses or other organizations because of the concrete nature of what they are selling. This can be an effective way to ease your volunteers into fundraising.

THINGS TO CONSIDER

As with many fundraising strategies, the first time you produce an ad book will be the hardest. However, if you produce an ad book annually, you will find that advertisers will renew their ads much more easily, the kinks of the design and printing process will be worked out, sample letters and solicitation materials will be ready, and a group of volunteers who have the experience of soliciting ads and producing an ad book will be in place. With each ad book produced, you will reap more rewards with less work.

You will need at least two or three volunteers to coordinate the sales, design, and production of the ad book. In addition, it is good to have at least two or three more volunteers to help solicit and follow up on ad sales and to distribute the ad book once it is printed.

An ideal amount of time to plan and produce the ad book is four months, especially if this is your first time.

Ad books can raise several thousand dollars if you have enough prospects to approach to buy an ad.

COSTS

The most significant costs will be printing and design, although you may have a volunteer who will donate design services. These are the costs involved:

- Design of ad book
- Printing
- Copying materials used to solicit ads
- Postage for ad book solicitation letters and for sending finished ad book to advertisers
- Long-distance phone calls for some ad solicitations

STEPS TO TAKE

These are the steps you should plan on taking. Each will be discussed in detail.

1. Make a plan and develop a budget
2. Recruit and train volunteers
3. Brainstorm a list of prospective advertisers
4. Develop a sales packet and mail or deliver it to prospects
5. Make follow-up calls and visits
6. Get the ad designs in
7. Produce the ad book
8. Distribute the ad book
9. Evaluate and send thank-yous

As you go through the steps in detail, use the sample workplan at the end of the chapter to create a timeline and task list.

Step 1: Make a Plan and Develop a Budget

With a strong prospect list you can expect to sell one ad for every three names on your list. Your budget should list projected income from ad sales and expenses. The cost of printing the ad book itself depends on the number of pages, quality of paper, and so forth, and can be as much as 70 percent of the entire cost for ad book production.

Your projected income depends on how many sales you can make and the prices you set for the ads. To set the prices for your ads, start by finding out what similar groups in your community charge in their ad books. Here's an example of pricing used by a small grassroots organization for an ad book with pages measuring 8½ by 11 inches:

One-line greeting (or listing of name): $50

Eighth page (or business-card size): $100

Quarter page: $175

Half page: $325

Full page: $600

Inside front or back cover: $800

Handout 12.1 shows sample sizes for an 8½ by 11-inch ad book page. If you're creating an ad book with these dimensions, you can give this handout to your prospective advertisers. Exhibit 12.1 shows a page from an ad book created to honor the twenty-fifth anniversary of the DataCenter.

If your organization has a Web site, consider whether you want to post your ad book on it; at the least you may want to acknowledge your advertisers there. When you solicit ads, an additional incentive would be acknowledgment or display of their ad on the Web site as well as in the program book.

Step 2: Recruit and Train Volunteers

The success of your ad book depends on the efforts of your volunteers. Selling ads is the heart of this project. If your volunteers have the materials and the support they need, the ad book can be very successful. Ideally, one person takes on the role of coordinator for ad sales. The coordinator provides the volunteers with materials (sales packet and tracking sheets) and the systems, training, and encouragement that they need. She also checks in weekly with all the ad solicitors to keep people working toward their goals and to help them solve problems that come up.

Here are some samples of what you can ask volunteers to do:

- Brainstorm prospective advertisers
- Write and design sales packet materials
- Solicit ads
- Follow up to get ad copy from advertisers
- Design ad book
- Work with printer
- Distribute ad book

See Resource A, Volunteer Recruitment Form, for help in identifying volunteers. Once you have your volunteer team, bring the volunteers together for at least one meeting to orient and train everyone on how to sell ads and to build a sense of connection to each other and to the project you're raising money for.

Here's a sample agenda for a volunteer training:

1. Introductions and icebreaker to set a relaxed and fun tone for the meeting. Icebreaker should be something quick, like going around the room saying your name, why you agreed to join this volunteer committee, and the best movie you saw recently.

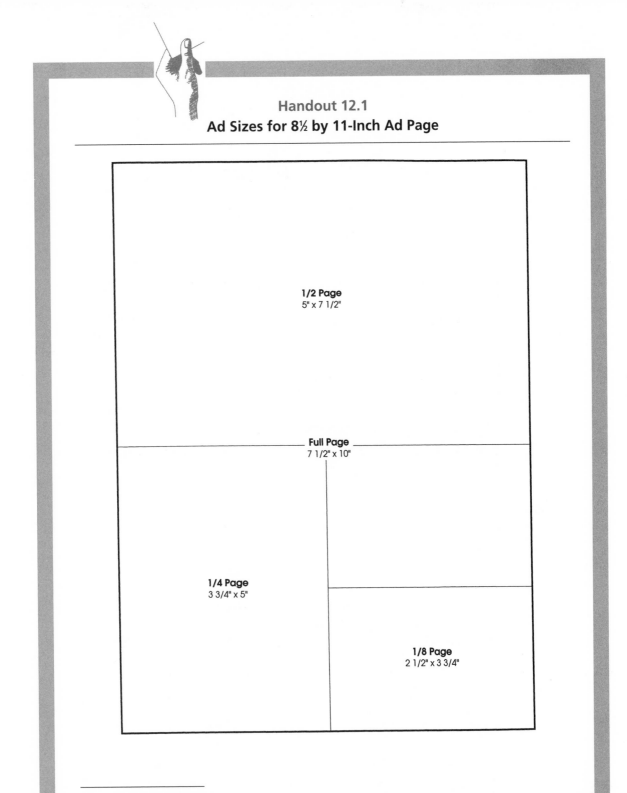

Handout 12.1
Ad Sizes for 8½ by 11-Inch Ad Page

1/2 Page
5" x 7 1/2"

Full Page
7 1/2" x 10"

1/4 Page
3 3/4" x 5"

1/8 Page
2 1/2" x 3 3/4"

Source: Courtesy of Mark Toney.

Exhibit 12.1
Sample Ad Book Page

Congratulations **Fred** and the entire staff of the **DataCenter** for twenty five years of a great organization.

Regards,

Leonard Merrill Kurz

Congratulations **25**

Center for Third World Organizing

CONGRATULATIONS DATACENTER !

FOR 25 YEARS OF PROVIDING IMPORTANT RESEARCH TOOLS AND TRAINING FOR ORGANIZING.

1218 East 21st Street
Oakland, CA 94606
Tel: (510) 533-7583
Fax: (510) 533-0923
www.ctwo.org

INKWORKS PRESS
2827 Seventh Street
Berkeley, CA 94710
(510) 845-7111
Fax (510) 845-6753
inkworks@igc.org
www.igc.org/inkworks

PROGRESSIVE PRINTING
WORKER-OWNED
UNION SHOP (SINCE 1974)
USING EXCLUSIVELY
SOY-BASED INKS
RECYCLED, CHLORINE-
FREE & TREE-FREE
PAPERS AVAILABLE

quality printing & design

There can be no *Social Justice* without *Economic Justice*.
Frederick Douglass

LAANE
LA Alliance for a New Economy

548 S. Spring St., Ste. 630 Los Angeles, CA 90013   (213) 486-9880 fax (213) 486-9886
info@laane.org   www.laane.org

CONGRATULATIONS, DATACENTER!

¡SI SE PUEDE!

AFSCME Local 3299
REPRESENTING 16,000 WORKERS
AT THE UNIVERSITY OF CALIFORNIA

Congratulations DataCenter

for 25 years of Research for Social Justice

Southwest Workers' Union
PO Box 830706 - San Antonio, TX 78283-0706
Phone: 210-299-2666 - Fax: 210-299-4009
Email: swu@igc.org - website: www.swunion.org

Source: Courtesy of DataCenter.

2. Explain the goals of the ad book: the fundraising goals, where the ad book will be distributed, what the money is being raised for, what advertisers will get out of placing an ad, and the types of people most likely to advertise in your book.

3. Review materials, including the list of people they'll be calling (and the form they'll be using to come up with additional prospects), tracking form, tips on selling ads, and sample letter.

4. Conduct role plays. Have people pair off and spend five or ten minutes practicing a follow-up call to potential advertisers. This is important, even for people who have sold ads before. Practice will help everyone get more familiar with the process of calling, the kinds of responses they might get, and how to handle those responses.

Step 3: Brainstorm a List of Prospective Advertisers

As with other fundraising strategies, your best prospects are people and businesses that you and people in your project already know. See Handout 12.2 for ideas for prospective advertisers.

Step 4: Develop a Sales Packet and Mail or Deliver It to Prospects

A packet should include the following items:

- A solicitation letter including the following information:

  The purpose of the ad book

  What the money is being raised for

  The number of ad books to be distributed and to whom

  What materials are included in the sales packet

  How to buy an ad

  The deadline for purchasing ads

  Whom to call for more information or to buy an ad

- An ad rate sheet that has a sample page of ads showing the ad sizes, prices, and layout possibilities

People who already know about your project or support you:

- Volunteers and supporters of your project
- Community organizations
- Family members
- Friends
- Colleagues at work
- People who are motivated but too busy to be involved

Local businesses and people who want to be known in the community:

- Restaurants
- Retail stores
- Accountants
- Real estate agents
- Self-employed people
- Elected officials
- People and organizations that advertise in other people's ad books
- Community resources
- Social service agencies

Places where you spend your money:

- Restaurants
- Corner store
- Rent, mortgage
- Car payments
- Video store
- Clothing
- Utilities
- Barbershop, beauty salon
- Hardware store
- Bank
- Grocery store
- Liquor store
- Gas station, auto repair shop
- Laundromat, dry cleaners
- Doctors
- Lawyers
- Accountants

Places where you spend time and interact with people:

- Workplace
- Church
- Community center
- Health club
- Bar, nightclub
- Bingo game
- Places where you volunteer
- School
- Union

Adapted from Mark Toney and the Center for Third World Organizing.

- An ad purchase form or ad book contract that states clearly how to purchase an ad and has places to indicate the size and rate being bought, additional buyer information, and instructions on how to provide ad copy or how to have an ad designed, including deadlines for submitting copy and any graphics
- Reply envelope to send ad purchase form and payment
- Optional: Any existing materials on your project, such as brochures, flyers, or newspaper clippings (but keep these to a minimum)

Here is a sample ad solicitation letter:

Dear Merchant:

Because you are someone who cares about the future of the youth of our community, we're writing to invite you to place an ad in our program book to celebrate the third anniversary of Y-MAD (Youth Making a Difference). The program book will include information about our programs, photos of the young people who have been involved in Y-MAD, and ads from a wide variety of local businesses, organizations, and other supporters. It will be distributed at our upcoming anniversary dinner, taking place on April 25.

Your contribution will help Y-MAD continue its work giving youth opportunities to develop new skills in solving community problems. More specifically, proceeds from our anniversary event and program book will sponsor twenty young people to participate in our summer internship program. For eight weeks during the summer, participants work in local community organizations where they learn about issues such as housing, health care, environmental justice, and violence against women. They also gain skills in organizing, membership recruitment, fundraising, media, and coalition building.

Your ad will reach more than five hundred people. We expect two hundred people to attend our anniversary event on April 25, where all of the guests will receive a copy of the ad book. In addition, we plan to send another three hundred copies of the book to our mailing list of friends and supporters in the community. We will also post the names of our ad buyers on our Web site, which receives several hundred hits in an average week.

Ad rates are listed on the enclosed form. They range from $50 for a one-line greeting to $800 for a full-page ad or $1,200 for a premium page (front or back of inside cover).

Please consider supporting the youth of our community by placing an ad. I will call you within the next week to discuss this request and answer any questions you may have.

Thank you for thinking about it!

Best wishes,

James Otis

Board Member

Exhibit 12.2 shows a sample purchase contract of the type mentioned in the letter.

Step 5: Make Follow-Up Calls and Visits

As with most other fundraising strategies, following up with personal contact is the most important step of the process. Very few people who receive the ad solicitation materials in the mail will respond without personal follow-up. Members of your volunteer team should call or visit the people and businesses who receive the sales packet one or two weeks after it is sent. The purpose of this follow-up is to make sure your prospects understand the purpose of the ad book and why you are raising money, to pitch why they should buy an ad, and to get their commitment to do so.

Ideally, you should match solicitors with prospects they know. If not, ask volunteers to just do a cold call or visit and go for it! A visit is especially useful when trying to get a local business to purchase an ad because face-to-face contact is always the most effective kind. Moreover, if the person asking is a customer, often the business owner or workers will recognize them even if they don't know their name or know to associate them with the project. This way, they can build on their customer or client relationship to get a commitment to buy an ad.

The solicitor should try to figure out who is the right person to speak to in order to sell the ad. Sometimes the volunteer will have to call back or return to speak to the manager or owner. Just remind them to be polite to everyone they encounter—not just out of common courtesy but also because the receptionist or other workers are often the gatekeepers to their manager or could have influence on the decision.

Exhibit 12.2
Sample Ad Book Contract

1996 CTWO Sixteenth Anniversary Adbook
-Adbook Contract-

Yes! I want to contribute to CTWO's fight for equal rights in education and employment for women and people of color by defending Affirmative Action in California, and across the U.S. The distribution of 4,000 Adbooks will begin at CTWO's 16th Anniversary Dinner on September 20, 1996 at the Scottish Rite Temple in Oakland, California.

☐ **Premium Page**	*Includes table for ten at dinner!*	$1200
☐ **Full Page**		$ 800
☐ **1/2 Page**		$ 400
☐ **1/4 Page**		$ 200
☐ **1/8 Page**		$ 100
☐ **Greeting**	*1 line, 8 words maximum.*	$ 50
☐ **Design Fee**	*Waived on camera ready ads..*	$15

Payment enclosed: Check # _____   Amount $ _____

Signature _____

Title _____

Organization _____

Address _____

City/Zip _____   Phone _____

Seller's Name: _____   Fax # _____

☐ **Please use my 1995 ad copy.**   ☐ **Camera ready ad copy enclosed.**

☐ **Include the following message:**   ☐ **Please design my ad.**

Please make a photocopy of contract and return original with your tax deductible check to:
CTWO • Center for Third World Organizing
1218 East 21st Street • Oakland, CA 94606 • (510) 533-7583 • Fax (510) 533-0923

Source: Courtesy of Mark Toney.

It is helpful to have a coordinator keep the sales process moving forward by making sure everyone has the materials, training, and motivation they need. Giving your sales team updates by e-mail or phone on the progress of the ad sales can help provide motivation and help people feel a part of a larger effort. You can even give prizes to the top number of ads sold and the highest dollar amount of sales. People who are behind in meeting their goals may be motivated to step up their efforts. The coordinator should also be a part of the team and set the pace by selling ads. Ad-sellers can use Worksheet 12.1, the Ad Sales Tracking Form, to manage their sales.

Script 12.1 is an example of a follow-up phone call.

Step 6: Get the Ad Designs In

Getting the actual ad from your advertisers is often the most time-consuming part of the process, especially when you are dealing with people who don't buy ads on a regular basis. At the time of the commitment, fill out the ad purchase form and mail the advertiser a copy, along with a thank-you note.

Here's a potential scenario:

February 25—You send a solicitation packet to the attention of Rochelle, your sales rep at Office Helper, the local office supply store with which you do a lot of business.

March 6—You follow up with a phone call to Rochelle. She isn't available, so you leave a message.

March 8—You call again. Rochelle doesn't remember receiving the packet, so you explain why you're calling. Rochelle asks that you send another copy of the materials and says she'll have to talk to the store manager. You send another packet out that day, indicating that you'll call back again in a couple of days and reminding her of the deadline for ad copy.

March 12—You call back; Rochelle says that her manager is thinking about it and will let you know within the week.

March 17—You haven't heard from Rochelle, so you call again. She's gone on vacation for the week and the manager is not available to speak to you.

March 25—Rochelle calls and says the store will take out a half-page ad and will get the copy to you by the following week (which is the deadline).

Worksheet 12.1
Ad Sales Tracking Form

Each time a call is made or updated information is obtained from a prospect, note it on this form. With all the details involved in putting together an ad book, it is important to keep track of your progress.

Name and contact info	Date letter sent	Date of follow-up call and result	Size and fee	Ad copy received date	Payment received date	Notes
Jo's Beauty Shop 123 First St. (424) 323-1234 jo@beautyshop.com	2/1	2/16—l.m. 2/23—thinking about it, call back 3/5—yes!	1/8 page, $100	3/25— reminder call 4/4—says will send by 4/10 4/12—ad rec'd	4/23— check rec'd	
Native American Health Center 600 Short St. (424) 321-8765 info@ nahc.net	2/1	2/16—send ltr again 2/28—has to talk to ED 3/5—needs more time 3/15—yes, but need us to design	1/4 page, $250	3/29—copy received and sent to designer		Will bring check to event

Script 12.1
The Follow-Up Call

Structure of what to say	What to say
Introduction	"Hello, may I speak to Jo? Hi, this is James Otis. I'm a board member of Youth Making a Difference, and I'm calling to follow up on a letter I sent you last week. Do you have a minute?"
If no	"When can I call you back?" (Mark on list when to call back and then do call.) If the prospect says, "I got your letter and we can't help you," say "Thank you" politely and hang up. (Mark "No" on list.)
If yes, explain why you're calling and engage the prospect	"As I explained in my letter, our group, Youth Making a Difference, is putting together an ad book as part of our upcoming third anniversary party. Are you familiar with our work?"
If yes, move directly to the ask	"I'm hoping you'll take out an ad in our book. In addition to showing your support for the important work we're doing with young people in our community, your ad will be seen by more than one thousand people."
If the prospect is not familiar with your group	"Youth Making a Difference got started because kids had so few opportunities to make a meaningful contribution to the community. We're now celebrating our third anniversary of doing work with middle-school and high-school youth. Nearly one hundred kids have gotten involved in community organizations and are learning how to be leaders. Do you have any questions about the project?"
Make the ask	"So, would you be willing to take out an ad in our program book?"
Stop and listen. Pause until they say something. If the answer is yes, they'll buy an ad	"Thank you so much! What size ad would you like?" Either refer them to the rate sheet with ad sizes that was sent with the letter or offer to send it again. Ask if they prefer to be sent an invoice because many businesses cannot pay you without one. Call back in a day or two. Remind them of the deadlines for submitting copy and payment.
If they say no	"Thank you for taking the time to talk to me. Can we call you at another time?"
If they say, "Maybe," or "I have to think about it," or "I have to talk to my business partner"	"I understand. Is there any additional information I could give you at this time to help with that decision?" and ask, "When is a good time for me to get back to you?"

April 1—Ad copy from Office Helper has not arrived, so you call Rochelle and learn that their ad designer was out sick and they need another couple of days. Rochelle also tells you that they realized they had overspent their advertising and contributions budget this year, so they will only want a one-quarter-page ad.

April 15—The day before the ad book is scheduled to go to the printer, your designer calls with the news that Office Helper's ad came in a program that her computer cannot open. You go to Office Helper to pick up a printed copy of the ad, which is the only way it will be in time to get in the ad journal. At 5:00 that afternoon, other groups have also not sent in their ad design despite rigorous follow up, so they have to be tracked down as well.

Although this scenario may seem like an exaggeration, these kinds of delays and challenges are actually quite common. The point here is that you should allow time for follow-up, prepare to be a bit of a nag, and have a good sense of humor. To minimize everyone's pain, the deadline for ad copy or design you give potential advertisers should be two weeks prior to the time your designer actually needs the ad copy. You may want to give groups the option from the beginning to have you design their ad—for a fee. In addition, it would be wise to have a note in your ad purchase form that if designs or copy are not received by a certain date, you will go ahead and make the design or copy for them. You can decide whether you want to add an additional design fee.

Step 7: Produce the Ad Book

Allow a month or more for the actual production phase—at least two weeks for the designer to lay out the ads and two weeks for printing. This time is especially important if a volunteer is doing the design. Exhibit 12.3 has a number of useful tips to follow in planning for your ad book.

Step 8: Distribute the Ad Book

If your ad book is being produced in conjunction with an event, make sure each member of the audience and all other event participants receive a copy. This is the least expensive and easiest way to get your ad book out. If the ads you have solicited are printed as part of a resource book, such as a directory or handbook, beyond distributing the book through the channels you normally would you might want to ask the businesses whose ads are in it to make it available to their members, customers, or clients.

> ### Exhibit 12.3
> ### Tips to Save Money (and Grief) in Producing Your Ad Book
>
> - Talk to your printer first about their requirements for the finished material you will send them. They're the best source for determining the format—that is, the software program—that will be easiest for them to work in. (Check with them on whether they can handle printed, "camera-ready" copy as well as electronic.) The printer will review the files you send them and may have additional requirements before going to print.
>
> - The most cost-effective page size for printing is a standard size—usually 8½ by 11 inches (if you want a smaller finished booklet, the pages can be laid out to be folded in half, to 5½ by 8½ inches).
>
> - For a book that is bound or folded, the total number of pages must be a multiple of four because a book or pamphlet is printed on both sides of a piece of paper that is folded in half or in quarters. Note that, for some printers, the kind of press they print on requires your total number of pages to be multiples of eight rather than four (eight, sixteen, twenty-four, and so on).
>
> - If any of your advertisers want to include photos, logos, or other graphic images, make sure the image is sent to you with a high enough resolution to come out clearly when you print it. Resolution of 300 dpi, at the size it will be printed on the page, is usually the minimum for a clear image to be produced.

Step 9: Evaluate and Send Thank-Yous

It is important that every advertiser in your ad book receive a copy of the ad book so they can see their ad and the product they put their money into. Along with the book, send a thank-you letter and any other promotional materials from your project that will tell them more about your work. Your thank-you and follow-up will build good will and make it possible, if you choose, to do another ad book or ask the advertiser to make a donation or in-kind contribution in the future.

Have a final meeting with your volunteers to evaluate how the process of doing the ad book went. Did you meet your income projections? Were there any unexpected expenses? Were there lessons that will be helpful to remember in the future? Be sure to file together a copy of the actual ad book, the contact information for all the advertisers, originals of all the materials you used, and contact information for the volunteers who helped with the ad book production. With one ad book under your belt, it will be much easier the next time you do an ad book. Moreover, you are likely to make more money the next time around because previous advertisers will already have said yes to buying an ad for your project. Thank all your volunteers, too, as they are the ones that made the ad book a success.

PICTURE THE HOMELESS

Picture the Homeless is an organization in New York City that is run by and for people who are homeless. They work on issues that their members identify as those most affecting their daily lives. Recently, the group produced its first ad book. With almost no staff involvement, the members solicited ads and produced the ad book, raising $2,000 after expenses. Their ad book included several pages of information about their work as well as six pages of ads. (Unfortunately, they had to pay an extra $1,000 in design fees when the designer was unable to open some of the files advertisers sent. They learned the hard way how important it is that you and your design person understand exactly what the requirements are, and what will happen with material that comes in a format the designer can't use.) Picture the Homeless was pleased that they raised as much as they did on this first-time effort. They are planning to do a second ad book with a goal of doubling their income from it.

WORKPLAN

The following workplan provides a summary of the key steps necessary to implement this fundraising strategy and an estimated time frame for each step. It is meant to be a template from which to create your own plan and your own timeline. By taking the time to create a plan and timeline, you'll be more organized, more likely to avoid last-minute crises, and ultimately more successful in raising the money you need.

Workplan 12.1
Ad Book

What	Who	1	2	3	4	5	6	7	8	9	10	11	12	13	14	15	16	Done
1. Make a plan																		
Decide what event or product ad book is for		x																
Make a budget—printer estimate, set ad prices		x																
Make a workplan		x																
Identify potential volunteer roles		x																
2. Recruit and train and volunteers																		
Recruit volunteers and match with roles and responsibilities		x	x															
Provide training and set goals			x															
Weekly check-in calls, support, sales updates				x	x	x	x	x	x	x	x	x						
3. Brainstorm prospective advertisers																		
Have volunteers brainstorm people to sell ads to			x															
Coordinate and match asks, size ad to ask for			x															
4. Develop and mail sales packet																		
Develop letter, ad rates sheet, ad purchase form, and so on			x	x														
Buy envelopes (letter and reply)			x															
Have mailing party					x													

What	Who	1	2	3	4	5	6	7	8	9	10	11	12	13	14	15	16	Done
										When (Week Number)								
5. Make follow-up calls																		
Make calls and get ad commitments					x	x	x	x	x	x	x							
Send out sales packets as needed					x	x	x	x	x	x								
Communicate results to coordinator, coordinator to give updates						x	x	x	x	x	x	x	x					
Coordinator sends out invoices and thank-yous to advertisers						x	x	x	x	x	x	x	x					
6. Get ad designs in																		
Make follow-up calls to get ad designs and payments							x	x	x	x	x	x	x					
Deadline for ad designs											x							
7. Produce ad book																		
Design ad book												x	x	x				
Deadline to send ad book layout to printer															x			
Printing															x	x		
8. Distribute ad book																	x	
9. Evaluate and send thank-yous																		
Send all advertisers ad book and thank-you																	x	
Evaluate ad book with volunteer team																	x	
Document ad book plan, materials, sales, ads, contacts																	x	
Send out thank-yous to volunteers																	x	

Car Washes

Car washes are an activity most people are familiar with. Holding one is a fairly simple and straightforward fundraising event. You find a location to hold the car wash and get materials and volunteers to donate their time; the money you collect from washing cars is donated to your project or organization. While a one-time car wash doesn't generally raise a large sum of money, it's popular among volunteers because it doesn't involve directly asking for money and it's popular among the public because people getting their cars washed are usually happy to support a cause, even though they may be just as interested in having a clean car.

If you hold your car wash for four to six hours in a location with a reasonable amount of traffic, charge $10 for the outside of the car and $15 for inside and out, you can expect to raise $400 to $500 in a day. If you have someone who has experience with car detailing, you can add waxing for an additional fee. Adding other components, such as a bake sale, will generate additional income.

BEST USES

A car wash works best when you have a small but enthusiastic group of, preferably, young people who are willing to get dirty washing cars. Car washes are a good choice if you don't have a big enough list of people you know to ask for a direct contribution, you need to raise some money quickly, and you're not necessarily trying to build a list of supporters for ongoing fundraising.

THINGS TO CONSIDER

You need a location that has outdoor access to water and, because of the oils and other toxics as well as the soap you wash the cars with, you need to have a method of safely disposing of the rinse water. (Some communities restrict the disposal of waste water, but even if yours doesn't, you don't want the water just running into the street, where it can pollute nearby water streams or sources.) The location should also be able to accommodate several cars at once.

Plan on having five to eight volunteers to wash the cars and a coordinator who deals directly with the customers and collects the money.

Weather is a major factor to consider in deciding to hold a car wash. Car washes work best in warmer months or climates and preferably when it's unlikely to rain.

One other consideration is whether you need liability insurance for this activity. One organization was sued by a customer who said his car was scratched at a benefit car wash. While this is probably not a particularly common occurrence, it's worth finding out what the costs and requirements for insurance are in your community.

COSTS

- Supplies for washing cars: soap, brushes, drying cloths
- Refreshments for volunteers
- Materials for publicity: signs, markers

STEPS TO TAKE

These are the steps you should plan on taking. Each will be discussed in detail.

1. Make a plan
2. Recruit volunteers
3. Find a location
4. Set a date
5. Decide on additional income-generating activities
6. Publicize the car wash
7. Make final preparations
8. Hold the car wash
9. Thank the volunteers

As you go through the steps in detail, use the sample workplan at the end of the chapter to create a timeline and task list.

Step 1: Make a Plan

Decide how much money you want to raise and, using the formula presented at the beginning of the chapter, how many volunteers you'll need and for how many hours. If volunteers are reluctant to commit to a whole day, consider having three two-hour shifts. Decide if this will be a one-time event or repeated on several different days (say, every Saturday for one month).

Step 2: Recruit Volunteers

Use Resource A, Volunteer Recruitment Form, to identify potential volunteers. Here are the things you'll ask them to sign up for:

- Find a location for the car wash
- Wash cars
- Get the materials for the day: soap, brushes, and so on
- Make signs
- Make flyers to distribute around town during the week before the car wash
- Post the event in free publications and on the Internet
- Send e-mail publicizing the event to everyone they know

Step 3: Find a Location

The best location for a car wash is on a busy street that has a lot of traffic going slowly enough that drivers have a chance to notice, slow down, and consider getting their car washed. Some groups have found a local gas station that is willing to let them set up a car wash on their premises. In that case, water for washing is available and you can approach people as they're pumping their gas. Others use the parking lot of a business or a school that is closed on Saturday.

Step 4: Set a Date

Find a time that will maximize participation from volunteers and customers. Saturdays are usually the best time for people to be willing to stop and get their cars washed. If you have enough people to help out, consider running the car wash over several weekends.

Step 5: Decide on Additional Income-Generating Activities

You can hold a bake sale at the same time as the car wash and invite drivers to purchase goodies while they're waiting for their car to be washed. A bake sale can bring in an additional $100 to $300. Or, if you're already organizing a raffle (see Chapter Fourteen), you can sell raffle tickets to the people getting their cars washed.

Step 6: Publicize the Car Wash

Although you're counting on the bulk of your business coming spontaneously from drivers who spot your car wash as they're passing by, you'll get even more business if people know about it ahead of time and plan to come because, in addition to a clean car, they want to help your cause. Post flyers in neighborhood businesses, take out inexpensive or free ads in community papers, and ask volunteers to send flyers and e-mails about the car wash to everyone they know. A sample flyer appears in Exhibit 13.1.

Step 7: Make Final Preparations

There are a number of things to do to get prepared for the day of the car wash:

- Get cash to make change and something to store it in.
- Prepare signs to hold up to catch the attention of drivers or to hang up if there's a place that will be noticed by people driving by.
- Prepare a sign-up sheet for anyone who wants more information about your project and is interested in being on your mailing list (get both e-mail and postal mail addresses).
- Make reminder calls to your volunteers.
- Get materials—soap, sponges, scrubbers, lots of towels to dry the cars and for volunteers to dry themselves off.
- Get refreshments for volunteers.

Step 8: Hold the Car Wash

If you're planning to run the car wash all day, schedule volunteers in two-hour shifts. Make it fun for them by having food and drink, and by rotating jobs— washing or rinsing, holding signs out encouraging drivers to stop, collecting the money.

Have someone available to talk to people who may want more information about the project or the organization you're raising money for. Offer any literature

Exhibit 13.1
Sample Car Wash Flyer

Come Get Your Car Washed

Saturday, June 3

9:00 A.M.–3:00 P.M.

in the parking lot of Eastside Elementary School

500 Main Street

to benefit the Campaign for Bilingual Education*

Prices:

- Basic Car Wash (exterior only): $8 (SUVs and trucks: $10)

- Full Treatment (wash and clean inside and out): $12 (SUVs and trucks: $15)

- Wax: $35 (SUVs and trucks: $50)

***** BAKE SALE TOO! Enjoy fresh-baked cookies, breads, pies, and more!*****

*The Campaign for Bilingual Education (CBE) is working to develop more Spanish-language immersion programs in our public schools in order to provide native English- and Spanish-speaking students with conversational and reading skills in both languages.

you may have and provide a sign-up sheet for anyone who wants to keep in touch about your work.

Step 9: Thank the Volunteers

Handwritten thank-yous are always appreciated by volunteers and will make them more likely to volunteer again in the future.

BENEFITS

Benefits, a program for recovering substance abusers, holds a weekly car wash on a busy street in Berkeley, California. As part of their community service requirement, the Benefits clients run the car wash, which takes place every Saturday from 10:00 A.M. to 3:00 P.M. They raise an average of $400 each week which, over the course of the year, brings in close to $20,000 for the program.

A CAR WASH PLEDGE EVENT

Diana Gomez, a music teacher at a public middle school in San Francisco, organizes an annual, one-day-only car wash as a fundraiser for the school's music department. What makes this car wash unusual—and financially very successful—is that it is organized as a pledge-raising event (see Chapter Ten, Bowlathons and Other Pledge-Raising Events). The students who are recruited to wash the cars ask people they know to sponsor them for each car that is washed that day. If, for example, someone pledges 5 cents per car, their donation comes to $10. The students set a goal of washing two hundred cars. About 250 students participate at various levels. Each student is asked to get a minimum of $25 in pledges. The cars are washed for free, and there is a donation box for people whose cars are being washed to make a contribution. In recent years, a bake sale has been added, which brings in additional funds. Now in its tenth year, this event raises about $12,000 from the pledges, another $1,000 in donations from people whose cars are washed, and $300 to $500 from the bake sale. Exhibit 13.2 shows a flyer for the event, and Exhibit 13.3 shows one child's sponsor sign-up sheet.

Exhibit 13.2
School Car Wash Flyer

Presidio Middle School
Music Department

Car Wash Fundraiser

Saturday, October 30   **9:00 A.M.–4:00 P.M.**

Dear Parents,

Enclosed in today's Wednesday Envelope is a packet of Music Department Car Wash Fundraiser papers. There's a pledge sheet for your child to keep track of sponsors. There is also a sample form letter for your child to use, with your permission. Should you decide to use the form letter, there are many more blank copies at school.

We have been having a successful Free Car Wash every year for the past ten years, often raising in excess of $12,000 per year. (If you want to know how we do that, just read the form letter!) This is the only Music Department fundraiser for the year. We hope your family will make a special effort to participate in whatever way possible.

Here's how you can help your child in this fundraiser:

Help line up sponsors.

Help send a few form letters to friends and relatives from out of town.

Send your child to help wash cars on Saturday, October 30.

Make a baked good for the bake sale on the day of the Car Wash.

Bring your car to be washed.

Come buy a delicious barbecue lunch at our "Polloderia" (chicken, rice, beans, tortilla, and soda for only $5!)

Sign up for one of the parent volunteer jobs. The sign-up sheets are posted outside the Music Rooms at Presidio. Or call 750-8435 (Mrs. Bottini, between 10:00 and 11:00 A.M.; Mrs. Gomez after 2:00 P.M.).

We hope this year's Free Car Wash Fundraiser will draw our music students together in a positive way, working to meet the year's budgetary concerns and having a lot of fun in the process!

Diana Gomez	Veronica Bottini
Band (ext. 3012)	Orchestra (ext. 3009)

Exhibit 13.3
Sponsor Sign-up Sheet

**PRESIDIO MIDDLE SCHOOL
MUSIC DEPARTMENT**

.... *FREE! CAR WASH!*

Saturday, October 30th
9:00 AM – 4:00 PM
29th Ave. at Geary Blvd.

Please Sponsor us! We plan to wash 200 Cars!!

Please come!

We are trying to raise money for musical instruments, sheet music, bus rental, and contest fees.

Will you please help us reach our goal of $5000 by being a sponsor for our Car Wash?

We plan to wash 200 cars! Which level would you like to support?

200 cars @ 1 cent per car: $2
200 cars @ 2 cents per car: $4
200 cars @ 5 cents per car: $10
200 cars @ 10 cents per car: $20
200 cars @ 25 cents per car: $50
200 cars @ 1 dollar per car: $200

Thank you for any amount you can donate. If you write a check, my teacher will mail a tax receipt to you. Please make your check payable to: **Presidio Student Body Funds-Music**

Thanks for your help! And remember to come get your car washed if you can!

Pledges Collected by: ___Nicholas Rojas___ Period ___333 Homeroom___

Name	Amount $20⁰⁰ SF	Paid
1.) Uncle Bruce Colville	65 Lisba St	✓
2.) Carmen Alonr	$4	✓
3.) Daleal Williams	$2	✓
4.) William Yuen	$2	✓

OVER →

WORKPLAN

The following workplan provides a summary of the key steps necessary to implement this fundraising strategy and an estimated time frame for each step. It is meant to be a template from which to create your own plan and your own timeline. By taking the time to create a plan and timeline, you'll be more organized, more likely to avoid last-minute crises, and ultimately more successful in raising the money you need.

Workplan 13.1
Car Wash

What	Who	When (Week Number)						Done
		1	2	3	4	5	6	
1. Make a plan		x						
Identify potential volunteer roles		x						
2. Recruit volunteers		x	x					
3. Find a location		x						
4. Set a date			x					
5. Plan additional fundraising activities (such as bake sale)		x						
6. Publicize				x	x	x		
7. Final preparations					x	x		
Reminder calls to volunteers					x	x		
8. Hold car wash						x		
9. Thank the volunteers							x	

Raffles

A common, easy, and fun way to raise almost any amount of money is a raffle. Almost everyone is familiar with raffles, having bought tickets for them and perhaps even won a prize in one. Because raffles are such a commonly used fundraising technique, most people don't realize that organizing one can be complicated. However, paying attention to the details involved will make a raffle both successful and fun for everyone involved.

Raffles basically appeal to people's desire to win something as well as to get something for less than it's worth. The way raffles work is that your organization gets some gifts donated that are then used as the prizes. These gifts may include cash, services such as child care for an evening or having your windows washed, or trips, DVD players, gift certificates, and so forth. Generally, there are five to ten prizes, one of which is a grand prize. Tickets are sold for between $1 and $10 each. Many more tickets are sold than prizes available, so there's an element of suspense and luck involved. At an appointed day and time, all the tickets are put into a barrel or other container, stirred up, and an uninvolved person, such as a child, draws out the winning tickets.

Aside from the tickets sold, there is no other source of income in a raffle. The costs can be kept low. Ideally, the only costs are printing the tickets and getting the prizes to the winners. As a result, most of the income is profit.

Material for this chapter has been adapted from Kim Klein, "How to Do a Raffle," in Kim Klein and Stephanie Roth (eds.), *Raise More Money: The Best of the* Grassroots Fundraising Journal (San Francisco: Jossey-Bass, 2001).

BEST USES

Raffles are good under the following circumstances:

- To bring in additional income as part of a special event (dinner, dance, party, and so on)

- When you're trying to raise money from people who are unlikely to give more than a small gift

- When the people you're trying to recruit to help raise money are shy about asking for money directly, but less frightened by the prospect of selling a inexpensive raffle ticket

- When you don't need to raise an enormous amount of money

- When you have a lot of people willing to sell tickets

THINGS TO CONSIDER

Raffles have to be organized carefully so that they don't violate gambling laws. Although laws prohibiting gambling are rarely enforced in regard to raffles, it's important to organize your raffle so that you are within the bounds of the law. In addition to federal and state laws, find out the laws in your community. Some communities require that you register with the sheriff's department; in communities where laws against raffles are strictly enforced you simply will not be able to do one. In California, for example, you are not allowed to use the word *raffle* at all; the acceptable terminology is "opportunity drawing."

The stickiest legal obstacle is that raffle tickets cannot actually be sold. We speak of "selling" tickets but actually what we should say is that the ticket is free and a donation of $1 (or whatever the amount determined) is requested. Technically, someone must be able to ask for and receive a ticket without giving you any money. Turning down such a request would be against the law. In this chapter, we refer to "selling" the tickets because that is the common shorthand; however, keep in mind that we are not truly selling anything.

One final word concerning the law: Many groups send raffle tickets to potential donors through the mail. This is against postal law and, if caught, your letters will be sent back. If you send tickets by bulk mail, you risk having your bulk mail permit revoked.

Another risk with raffles is that, because people are handling small amounts of money, almost always cash, it's easy for ticket sellers to lose track of how many tickets they've sold and how much cash they've collected. See Step Seven for ideas of how to minimize the number of tickets and cash that disappear, but also assume that you will never get 100 percent return on the tickets you distribute to volunteers.

COSTS

- Printing of raffle tickets
- Photocopying
- Postage (for solicitation letters, sending tickets to sellers, and sending out prizes)

STEPS TO TAKE

These are the steps you should plan on taking. Each will be discussed in detail.

1. Make a plan
2. Recruit volunteers
3. Solicit prizes
4. Design and print tickets
5. Distribute tickets to volunteers
6. Motivate volunteers to keep selling
7. Collect tickets and money
8. Hold the drawing
9. Send out prizes and thank-yous and evaluate

As you go through the steps in detail, use the sample workplan at the end of the chapter to create a timeline and task list.

Step 1: Make a Plan

First, set your fundraising goal. If you have decided to sell your raffle tickets for $1 each, for example, with a packet of six going for $5, then make your calculations assuming that most people will buy a packet of tickets. So, to raise $1,000, you'll need to sell about two hundred packets, for a total of twelve hundred tickets. Assume, too, that a volunteer can sell about ten packets of tickets over the course of the raffle. Use that formula as a way to estimate how many people you need to recruit to sell tickets. To sell two hundred packets, then, you need twenty people selling.

There are two other elements your plan should include:

- Where the drawing will take place. Will the raffle drawing be part of a larger event or party, or will you just bring the people who worked on the raffle together for a celebration and do the drawing there? Either one will work; making the drawing part of a larger event allows you to sell more tickets at the event itself.

- Potential prizes and who might donate them.

Step 2: Recruit Volunteers

In addition to selling tickets, which is the task you most want to recruit volunteers to do, here are some other tasks you might want to ask people to help carry out. Use the Volunteer Recruitment Form in Resource A to come up with a list of potential volunteers and what you'll ask them to do.

- Draft solicitation letter for prizes
- Identify potential prize donors
- Solicit prizes
- Design and print tickets
- Recruit more ticket sellers
- Motivate ticket sellers
- Help organize the drawing
- Thank everyone who helped out

In thinking about possible ticket sellers, consider people who work in large office buildings or unions, or who have large families or a large circle of friends. Raffles are a good opportunity to get some peripheral people involved, so don't just go to your reliable volunteers who already do everything else. Ask each person if they know someone who would be good at selling tickets. People's spouses or partners, neighbors, business partners, and the like, can be recruited for this effort. You want to have as many ticket sellers as you can possibly find, both to distribute as many tickets as possible and also because some people who sign up to sell tickets will end up not doing so. Offer a prize for the person who brings in the most money selling tickets. (You may also want to award other small prizes to ticket sellers as a way to encourage sales, as described in step 8.)

Step 3: Get the Prizes

It is helpful if the prizes have a theme, such as vacations, services, electronics, household, or restaurants. Make a list of all the vendors who might donate a prize, and list specifically what you want from them, such as dinner for two, a weekend cabin, and so on. Remember that people who own small businesses, particularly those in storefronts, frequently get asked to donate raffle prizes. They may have policies against doing it; they may have donated to five other charities and are not taking on any more; they may be having a hard time in their business and not be inclined to give you anything. For those reasons, it is good to have at least three times as many potential sources of prizes as prizes needed.

Assign volunteers to solicit the prizes. In some cases, with people they know, a volunteer can just make a phone call and follow up with a letter if the prospect agreed to donate something. In other cases, they might want to send a short letter first, stating what they'd like the person to donate and what cause or organization the raffle is supporting. Stress to each merchant how many people will see the tickets, how much other publicity you are going to do, that you will not ask for another item this year, or whatever is true for you. Merchants must think about how giving your organization an item is good for their business, and you must help them in that thinking. You will have greater success getting prizes from merchants that you know personally, that your organization does business with, or that you know believe in the cause you're raising money for. So start with them.

Use Handout 14.1 to assist you in identifying potential donors.

When thinking about raffle items to solicit, remember to ask your team of volunteers what *they* can offer, as well as who they know who might be able to contribute something. Think, too, about whom your organization does business with and whether they might be a potential source of an auction item. Here are some ideas.

Gift certificates from local retailers:

- Bookstores
- Sporting goods stores
- Clothing stores
- Restaurants
- Movie theaters

Services:

- Massages
- Haircuts
- Home-cooked dinner
- Babysitting

Vacations:

- Airline tickets
- Frequent-flyer miles
- Night at a bed and breakfast

Classes or personalized instruction:

- Foreign-language instruction
- Music lessons
- Knitting, sewing, gardening
- Self-defense
- Yoga, tai chi, or the like

Things people like:

- DVD player
- Television
- Electronic organizer
- Basket of skin care products or small food items
- Home-baked cakes, cookies, pies
- Cash

Exhibit 14.1 shows a sample donation form to use with donors. If you send or drop off a letter, include a donor form that your prospects can fill out to indicate what they're contributing.

The Raffle Prize Tracking Form in Worksheet 14.1 will help volunteers keep track of who they've asked and what prizes have been committed.

For volunteers who are approaching potential donors with a letter, the following sample letter soliciting raffle prizes will give them an example of what it can say.

> Dear Friend (or Merchant):
>
> I'm writing as a volunteer with Healthy Farmers, Healthy Communities to ask you to help us with our project to bring a weekly farmer's market to our neighborhood. The market will be located in the empty lot on the corner of Fifth and Grove streets, and we are looking to raise $2,000 to clean up the lot and publicize the market to the community. We have commitments from several local farmers who are interested in selling their produce at a Saturday market and we think there will be a lot of interest from the community.
>
> One of the ways we are raising money is through a raffle. We hope you would be willing to donate an item or service to this project.
>
> We believe that having a local place to purchase good, fresh produce will bring more customers into town, which will also benefit small businesses like yours. As you know, many residents of our community end up shopping in the malls outside of town. A weekly farmer's market will benefit all of us: local farmers, small businesses, and the people who live here.
>
> If you can contribute something to this fundraising effort, please fill out and return the enclosed donation form. We greatly appreciate whatever you can give.
>
> I will be calling to follow up on this letter within the next week and to answer any questions you may have.
> Sincerely,
> (Name and Position)

Step 4: Design and Print the Tickets

Once you have the prizes, decide which will be the grand prize, the second prize, and so on, so you can feature the top prizes in the ticket design. Designing the tickets

Exhibit 14.1
Sample Donation Form

Healthy Farms, Healthy Communities

Raffle Donation Form

Thank you for your contribution of a prize to HFHC's upcoming raffle. Please complete this form and return it to the address below no later than March 1.

Donation: Please describe your donation for listing on the raffle ticket, for example, "DVD player," "Dinner for two at Chez Moi," "$100 gift certificate to Sally's Spa." Please indicate if there are any restrictions on the prize, such as limited time availability or other special instructions.

_____

_____

_____

☐ Items or gift certificates included

☐ Please make up a gift certificate for me

☐ I will send or deliver my donation by March 1

☐ Please send a volunteer to pick up my donation

Offer expiration date: _____   Retail value: $_____

Important! The donor name shown below will be acknowledged in publicity about the raffle. If the donor wishes to remain anonymous, please check here: _____

_____ Business donor _____ Individual donor

Donor Name _____

Contact Name (if business donor) _____

Mailing Address _____

City, State, ZIP _____   E-Mail _____

Day Phone _____   Evening Phone _____

Donor Signature _____   *Date* _____

Please return the completed form by March 1 to HFHC c/o Ralph Henderson, 45 Chestnut St., Chattanooga, TN 37000.

Worksheet 14.1
Raffle Prize Tracking Form

Name and contact info	Type of prize	Who will solicit and how?	Date solicitation made (and how)	Result	Next steps and comments
Eli's Electronics 123 First St. (424) 234-4321	DVD player	Rashid (will send letter and visit)	10/12—letter sent		Will go to store and talk to Eli
Miriam Jacobs Coco's Café 35 Central Ave. (424) 999-1010	Dinner for two	Johanna (letter and phone call)	10/20—sent letter 10/30—called, l.m. 11/4—called	Miriam said maybe	Johanna will call her in a week

requires attention to a number of details. Refer to Exhibit 14.2 for a sample of what should go on the tickets.

There are a few phrases that must be printed on the ticket and others that are a good idea to have there. The first two in the following list are required:

- How to get a free ticket (this can be in small type).

- List of winners supplied on request. (This is to help ensure that the prizes are actually awarded.)

- The donor doesn't have to be present to win. (This will help increase sales.)

- A ticket number. (This will make it easier to keep track of the tickets you have handed out to volunteers to sell. Although it may cost more to have numbers printed on the tickets, it is worth it.)

It is also critical that the ticket stub be perforated so it can be easily separated from the body of the ticket. This is another worthwhile expense. Don't try to save money by printing cheap raffle tickets. Your volunteers will not distribute them as easily and donors will be reluctant to give their money when the ticket does not appear properly done.

Because of the need for numbering and perforation, not all printers can print raffle tickets. Find a printer who can. Of course, seek to have the printing donated, but don't scrimp on printing costs. Notice on the sample ticket that the seller is asked to sign his or her name on the ticket stub. This gives you a way to know how many tickets each volunteer sold (this could be helpful information if you decide to do a raffle again or if you're looking for enthusiastic fundraising volunteers). It also gives you a way to keep track of ticket sales for the incentive prize to the person who sold the most tickets.

To keep track of who buys tickets, not only so you can contact them if they win a prize, but also so you can go back to them at a later date to ask for their support again, instruct the ticket sellers to make sure that addresses, phone numbers, and where appropriate, e-mail addresses are on the ticket stubs they turn in.

To promote the organization holding the raffle, also include a box the purchaser can check to get more information about the group's work. If you do make such an offer, be sure you go through all the tickets, pull out those with checked boxes, and send the information in a timely manner.

To know how many tickets to print, add up how many tickets your volunteer workers are willing to take and compare that with your goal for the raffle, then make

Exhibit 14.2
Sample Raffle Ticket

No. 4467

Name _____

Address _____

City _____

State _____ ZIP _____

☐ Please send me more information on Healthy Communities.

Seller's name _____

- -

HEALTHY COMMUNITIES ANNUAL RAFFLE

Suggested Donation: $1.00 per ticket, 6 tickets for $5.00

Grand Prize: Trip for two to Paris!

Second Prize: Laptop computer

Third Prize: $250 cash

A benefit for Healthy Communities

DRAWING: December 10, 2005

You need not be present to win. Free ticket available on request. Winners will be notified by mail. For a list of winners, submit a self-addressed stamped envelope.

Address correspondence to Healthy Communities, 201 First Street, Chattanooga, TN 37000.

No. 4467

appropriate adjustments, as needed. Print at least 10 percent more tickets than you need to reach your financial goal, as some tickets are bound to be lost or mutilated.

Step 5: Distribute and Keep Track of the Tickets

Make a list of everyone selling tickets and the number ranges of the tickets they take. Then, using a form such as Worksheet 14.2, keep track of the ticket stubs as they are returned.

Ticket sales should go on for at least one month, and can continue for two to three months. After two or three months you'll lose momentum and you may also have a harder time collecting the money.

Step 6: Motivate Volunteers to Keep Selling

Call your volunteers at least once a week to see how they are doing with their ticket sales. Remind them of the deadline and ask that they send in stubs and cash as these accumulate. If they aren't selling as many tickets as they expected to, ask them what kind of support they need. Let them know how all the other ticket sellers are doing in order to encourage them to keep going. Tell them who is winning the "most sold" prize so far.

One member of the team, the raffle coordinator, should be responsible for making sure people have enough tickets to sell and that they are in fact selling them. Raffles fail when there are not enough people selling tickets or when the people who take tickets don't sell them. Praise those who are doing their job and encourage those who aren't.

Every volunteer ought to be able to sell a minimum of twenty-five individual tickets, or ten packets of ten tickets each. Most people who live in a relatively populated area can sell fifty tickets in two or three weeks with no difficulty. Some people will be able to sell one hundred—and even up to five hundred—tickets in one or two months.

Step 7: Round Up the Tickets and Money

Surprisingly, most groups find that the most difficult task in a raffle is not in getting the prizes or the workers, but getting the tickets and the cash back from the sellers.

Some volunteers will be careless with their ticket stubs, or they will return stubs and promise cash later, or they may claim to have sold tickets when they really

Worksheet 14.2
Raffle Ticket Tracking Form

Name _____*Young Min*_____ Number of tickets taken __100__ Date __4/25__

Check-in calls or e-mails	Date	Number of tickets sold	Funds collected ($)	Unsold tickets returned	Funds turned in ($)
	5/8	20	$20		
	5/22	54	$45		
Total:		74	$65	Total: _26_	$65

Name _____ Number of tickets taken _____ Date _____

Check-in calls or e-mails	Date	Number of tickets sold	Funds collected ($)	Unsold tickets returned	Funds turned in ($)
	____	____	____		
	____	____	____		
Total:	____	____	____	Total: _____	_____

Name _____ Number of tickets taken _____ Date _____

Check-in calls or e-mails	Date	Number of tickets sold	Funds collected ($)	Unsold tickets returned	Funds turned in ($)
	____	____	____		
	____	____	____		
Total:	____	____	____	Total: _____	_____

Name _____ Number of tickets taken _____ Date _____

Check-in calls or e-mails	Date	Number of tickets sold	Funds collected ($)	Unsold tickets returned	Funds turned in ($)
	____	____	____		
	____	____	____		
Total:	____	____	____	Total: _____	_____

haven't. If you have encouraged people to turn in money and stubs as they go along, you will have less difficulty than if you wait to collect all the stubs and proceeds until just before the drawing. Final submission of stubs and cash—and unsold tickets—should be due at least three days, and preferably five days, before the drawing. That way, you can ensure that you have all the tickets accounted for well ahead of time. Another advantage of getting ticket stubs in well ahead of time is that some people try to make their stub into the winning one by bending down a corner, sticking something on the back, or tearing it nearly in half and then taping it together. Workers will sometimes fold ticket stubs or spill stuff on them. These stubs cannot be used, and new stubs must be written. This is, in part, the use of the two hundred or so extra tickets. For the drawing, the stubs must be as uniform as possible.

Step 8: Hold the Drawing

The drawing is held on the date printed on the ticket, either as part of another event such as a dance or auction, or in a ceremony of its own. It's fine to have a small party for all those who worked on the raffle and sold tickets and do the drawing there. If you have good food and drink, the drawing is then a celebration and a reward for a job well done, as well as a way to ensure that all the sold tickets are turned in on time.

Get a big box or barrel for the ticket stubs. Mix and remix the stubs thoroughly after each prize is drawn. Start with the last prize and work up to the grand prize.

After the winning ticket stubs are drawn, announce the prizes for top salespeople and award these. Many organizations give several prizes to their salespeople. In addition to the person who sold the most tickets, they award a prize to the person who got the most prizes donated, the person who got the most other people to sell tickets, the person who sold the most tickets in a week or the most to a single person, and so on. Having a lot of prizes for salespeople is a good motivator for those who are competitive during the selling process and a nice reward at the end.

Aside from finding who wants more information about your group, you may want to use the ticket stubs to get names and addresses for a mail appeal or e-alert later. Although it can be labor intensive to sort through the ticket stubs to garner this information (while eliminating the names of current members or anyone already on your mailing list), this is a productive way to build a good mailing list.

Step 9: Send Out the Prizes and Thank-Yous and Evaluate

Arrange for the winners to get their prizes, either by picking them up at your office or receiving them in the mail.

Send a thank-you note to each person who sold tickets and to all the merchants and others who donated prizes.

Count your money. Note how many tickets were unsold, any problems there were with the workers, the merchants, the tickets themselves, and so on. Make a file with all the information about the raffle, including lists of winners, people donating items, volunteers, and any notes about timing and other issues. If you decide to do another raffle in the future, it will be much simpler if a committee can pull out the file and benefit from your prior experience.

NEIGHBORS IN MINISTRY

Neighbors in Ministry is an organization in Brevard, North Carolina, that runs an after-school program called Rise and Shine Freedom School. They raised $500 for their program in just two weeks through a "Back to School Shopping Spree" raffle. They printed a total of one thousand tickets and sold them for $1 each. There was only one prize—a cash gift of $500—which made the tickets easy to sell. A total of forty parents and ten board members each sold twenty tickets, bringing in $1,000, which was split evenly with the winner.

WORKPLAN

The following workplan provides a summary of the key steps necessary to implement this fundraising strategy and an estimated time frame for each step. It is meant to be a template from which to create your own plan and your own timeline. By taking the time to create a plan and timeline, you'll be more organized, more likely to avoid last-minute crises, and ultimately more successful in raising the money you need.

Workplan 14.1
Raffle

What	Who	1	2	3	4	5	6	7	8	9	10	11	Done
1. Make a plan													
Make a budget		x											
Decide if stand-alone or part of event		x											
2. Recruit volunteers			x										
Prepare materials													
Orient volunteers				x									
Come up with ideas for raffle prizes													
Draft forms and sample letters				x									
3. Solicit raffle prizes					x	x	x						
Make follow-up calls to volunteer solicitors					x	x	x						
4. Design and print tickets						x	x						
5. Distribute tickets to volunteers							x	x	x	x	x		
6. Follow up with ticket sellers								x	x	x	x		
7. Collect money and ticket stubs								x	x	x	x		
8. Hold the drawing											x		
9. Send out prizes and thank-yous and evaluate											x	x	

Garage Sales

I t's hard to find a person living in the United States who hasn't held one, bought something at one, or at the very least walked or driven by one. Garage sales—also called tag sales, stoop sales, sidewalk sales, or rummage sales—are popular because they epitomize the old saw that one person's trash is another person's treasure. They are also easy to organize, and with a little extra time and planning, their fundraising potential can be increased by involving more and more people in the activity. A community in San Francisco has an annual neighborhood-wide garage sale in which more than 150 families participate.

This chapter describes how to organize a garage sale in which you solicit contributions of items to sell from as many people as you can manage and hold the sale in a public setting such as a community center or playground.

BEST USES

Garage sales do not require people who come to buy things to be committed to the cause you're raising money for. Therefore, if you don't have a lot of prospects who might make contributions in response to a mail appeal or personal solicitation, or who would attend a house party or other event, you can still raise money through this kind of activity. To raise more than a couple of hundred dollars, however, consider getting several households involved as well as choosing a location that gets a lot of passersby.

THINGS TO CONSIDER

Items to be sold should be in good condition, not broken or damaged things that are unlikely to sell easily. Think about where you'll store the donated items in the days (or weeks) leading up to the sale, and remember that you'll have to find some way to dispose of all of the unsold items at the end of the day. These considerations may cause you to limit the size of items you ask to be donated.

Garage sales can be organized in just a few weeks. However, plan on six to eight weeks' lead time if you want to recruit lots of people to help out and if you want to publicize the sale beyond your immediate neighborhood.

COSTS

- Rental of place to hold the sale
- Rental of tables to display items
- Publicity
- Refreshments for volunteers
- Stickers for pricing items

STEPS TO TAKE

These are the steps you should plan on taking. Each will be discussed in detail.

1. Make a plan
2. Recruit volunteers
3. Find a location for the sale
4. Solicit donations of items to sell
5. Publicize the sale
6. Make final preparations
7. Hold the sale
8. Wrap up
9. Thank volunteers and people who donated items to sell

As you go through the steps in detail, use the sample workplan at the end of the chapter to create a timeline and task list.

Step 1: Make a Plan

Set a goal for how much money you want to raise, then determine how many people you need to ask for donations. Assume that each person will donate enough items to bring in $50, on average. If, for example, you want to raise $1,000, then plan to have donations from at least twenty people.

Step 2: Recruit Volunteers

Use the Volunteer Recruitment Form in Resource A to help identify potential volunteers. You'll be recruiting people for the following tasks:

- Find a location for the garage sale
- Solicit contributions of items for the sale
- Arrange to have donated items picked up or dropped off
- Store items ahead of time (if they can't be held at the sale location)
- Publicize the sale
- Organize and price items; set up tables the morning of the sale
- Cashier during the sale, circulate and help customers, straighten up the sales tables throughout the day

Step 3: Find a Location to Hold the Sale

Consider the best location in your community that will draw a lot of impulse shoppers. You'll need a space large enough to accommodate the number of items you're selling that's also visible to passersby. The summer months, or any time of the year when people are out in the streets more, are the best times to hold a garage sale. If there is a risk of poor weather, look for an indoor space such as a community center, school gym, or church community room to hold the sale.

Step 4: Solicit Donations of Items to Sell

Ask everyone you know to consider donating items to the sale. Ask them also to spread the word to people they know. E-mail is a great medium for getting the word out, and an e-mailed request can get to hundreds of people within hours.

Give people examples of the kinds of things that you would like them to donate to the sale. The best items are dishes, silverware, lamps, and anything that a student or person moving into their first house or apartment might need. Tools such as shovels, saws, hammers, and so on also sell well. Books can sell well if they are priced to move and people are encouraged to buy several at once (with enticements such as discounts for purchasing more than one book). Furniture, especially desks, chairs, sofas, and outdoor furniture in good shape will sell if you advertise what you have. If you have things requiring electricity, such as toasters, microwave ovens, computers, and so on, make sure that they are working ahead of time and note that on the item; it's also good to provide a way to for someone to plug the item in and test it for themselves. Discourage donations of clothes, unless they're baby clothes in good condition, because they don't usually sell well.

If you get donations of valuable items such as antiques, good furniture, or almost-new electronic equipment—anything that would sell for more than $100— don't include them in the garage sale, but sell them at an online auction site such as eBay. If you anticipate having a lot of valuable things, you may want to ask an antique dealer or an estate sale expert to look over your items and tell you which ones may be worth more than most people will pay in a garage sale. There are many instances of estate-sale experts finding rare books, dolls, vases, and even stamp or coin collections that are worth more by themselves than most of the other stuff put together.

Keep in mind the need to store the donated items before the sale. You'll be surprised at how much space they take up in your basement or living room.

Step 5: Publicize the Sale

Although you're counting on some of your business coming from people who happen to walk or drive by, you'll get even more customers if people know about the sale ahead of time, especially those who may want to help your cause in addition to the possibility of getting some good bargains. Publicize the sale by posting flyers in neighborhood businesses, taking out inexpensive or free ads in community papers, sending e-mails to everyone you know, and employing other standard ways of notifying people of the sale. There are people who go to garage sales regularly and are serious shoppers. As shown in Exhibit 15.1, include in your publicity the kinds of items you have, such as "Infant and baby clothes and furniture," "Several almost complete sets of dishes," or "Everything a gardener could need."

Step 6: Make Final Preparations

It's helpful to make yourself a checklist of things to do in the few days leading up to the sale. Here are some things to include:

- Get cash to make change and a cashbox to keep the money in. Be sure you have a calculator and a receipt book for anyone who wants a receipt.

Exhibit 15.1
Sample Flyer

Fabulous Benefit Garage Sale!

Saturday, September 14th
9:00 A.M. – 3:00 P.M.

at Lakeside Community Center
500 Main Street

to benefit *Restore Our River**

Furniture!

Dishes & cookware!

Books & CDs!

Great Prices!

Electronics!

*__Restore Our River__ is working to get the Noxious Chemical Corp to clean up the polluted Clearwaters River, where they dumped toxic waste for twenty years. In 2002 legislation was passed prohibiting these practices. Proceeds from this garage sale will help us keep the pressure on Noxious Chemical to clean up the river.

- Mark each item's price with a tag that will stay on and is easy to see. Price things slightly or well below their market value. The goal here is to get all the items sold. Profit in a garage sale is from volume.

- Prepare signs to post at the sale both to catch people's attention and to publicize that the sale is a fundraiser.

- Prepare a sign-in sheet for anyone who wants more information about your project (which is also a way to get new names for your mailing list if you're going to be doing ongoing fundraising).

- Make reminder calls to your volunteers.

- Have food and drink available for the volunteers.

Step 7: Hold the Garage Sale

The following guidelines will help you have a successful garage sale:

- Have everything set up by 8:00 A.M. The serious shoppers will already be at your sale by 7:30 or 8:00. Do *not* let anyone into the sale until you are open no matter how much they beg and plead.

- As a reward for volunteering, you may want to let the volunteers have first dibs on items for sale either the night before or in the morning before the sale opens.

- Give volunteers a badge or a T-shirt of your organization to wear so that buyers can easily identify who can answer questions.

- In a big sale, have a volunteer stationed at every corner or by each table so that the volunteers can watch all that is happening all the time. Surprisingly, people will shoplift, but the presence of volunteers will discourage them.

- Volunteers should continuously straighten things up and keep the garage sale site tidy and inviting.

- Two people should always stand by the cash box and every hour or so, one of them should take large bills and checks to a secure location.

- Authorize volunteers to lower the price of any single item by 10 percent and multiple items by 20 to 25 percent. After noon, volunteers can lower the price of any single item by 20 percent and multiple items by 50 percent. At the end of the day, they can lower prices as much as they want in order to move everything out. However, for people who try to bargain hard, the volunteer should stress that the sale is for a good cause and be willing to hold out for more money. Ideally, your volunteers are people who love garage sales themselves and so are familiar with the strategies buyers sometimes have of insulting the items ("I would have thrown this in the trash" or "This is going to need a lot of work") or insulting the pricing structure ("I have never seen prices like these. It's a tag sale, for heaven's sake"). You may want to have one volunteer who is authorized to make big deals, for example, if someone offers to buy all the books you have.

- Most volunteers should be relieved after two or three hours, though some who love sales may be happy to stay all day. Most people will want to shift jobs so that they can look over all the items over the course of the day.

- Leave the place at least as clean as when you came. Pick up all litter, and don't fill the trash cans or Dumpsters to the brim.

Step 8: Wrap Up

Because you're dealing with a lot of cash, it's a good idea to have at least two people count the money and prepare the bank deposit. Ideally, you will deposit the money the same day. If that is not possible, lock the cash in a safe place until you can deposit it, but make sure that more than one person knows how much cash has been taken in.

Make arrangements to donate any leftover items in good condition to your local nonprofit thrift store. In some cases, they will come pick them up from you.

If you think you may want to make this an annual event, jot down what worked well and what didn't, where the sale was held, how many volunteers were needed, how much money was raised, and anything else that might be helpful for someone else organizing such a sale for your group next year or in the future.

Step 9: Send Thank-Yous

Send thank-you notes to everyone who donated items to the sale and to everyone who volunteered in any capacity.

THE BERNAL HEIGHTS NEIGHBORHOOD CENTER SALE

The Bernal Heights Neighborhood Center in San Francisco has been holding a neighborhoodwide garage sale for the past twelve years. Their method is to recruit residents of their community to hold a garage sale at each of their homes on a designated day in August. The first year they organized the event, about twenty families participated. Twelve years later, 160 families held garage sales. Families are charged a flat fee of $25 and keep the proceeds of their sale. Some decide to give a percentage of the proceeds from their sales to the neighborhood center. The center publicizes the event, prepares a map with the locations of the garage sales, and hosts its own garage sale for people who just want to donate a few items but not hold their own sale. This sale has become an enormous community event, with people coming from all over the city and the entire Bay Area to shop for bargains. Although the fundraising aspect of the event is not significant—net income last year was about $4,800—it has helped the center build relationships with the community and increase its presence in the neighborhood.

WORKPLAN

The following workplan provides a summary of the key steps necessary to implement this fundraising strategy and an estimated time frame for each step. It is meant to be a template from which to create your own plan and your own timeline. By taking the time to create a plan and timeline, you'll be more organized, more likely to avoid last-minute crises, and ultimately more successful in raising the money you need.

Workplan 15.1
Garage Sale

What	Who	When (Week Number)							Done
		1	2	3	4	5	6	7	
1. Make a plan									
Set fundraising goal and create budget		x							
Identify potential volunteer roles		x							
2. Recruit volunteers			x	x					
3. Find a location			x						
Finalize location and date				x					
4. Solicit donated items to sell			x	x	x	x	x		
Find place to store items (before sale)				x	x				
Arrange for item dropoffs or pickups				x	x	x	x		
5. Publicize sale					x	x	x		
6. Make final preparations						x	x		
7. Hold the sale							x		
8. Wrap up							x		
9. Send thank-yous								x	

CONCLUSION

We hope that by now you're excited to try one or more of the fundraising strategies described in this book. We hope, too, that you can see that fundraising is by its nature a community-building activity that not only brings in much-needed cash for the causes we believe in, but also expands the networks of people who learn about important social or neighborhood issues and join in making a difference in the world. Your work deserves the financial support you can round up—whether you're planting trees, stopping toxic waste dumping, providing emergency relief after a natural disaster, keeping schools open, standing up to injustice, or organizing recreational programs for kids. The information provided here for how to carry out a diverse range of fundraising activities is based on the real-life experiences of thousands of people, projects, and organizations throughout North America. Following the instructions in this book, you can join them in creating your dream of a better world.

We wish you great fundraising success—and fun in getting there!

Resources

Worksheet A.1
Volunteer Recruitment Form

resource
A

Use this worksheet to identify potential volunteers for your fundraising project.

(1) Name and contact info (address, phone, e-mail)	(2) Relationship to you or the organization	(3) What will you ask them to do?[a]	(4) Recruitment call made (date and outcome)	(5) Other[b]

[a]Refer to the chapter that describes the strategy you'll be carrying out. Each description includes a list of tasks that you'll want to recruit volunteers to help out with. Use that list to come up with items for column 3.

[b]Use this column for relevant information about this person: language skills, experience such as graphic design, fundraising, computer skills, and so on.

If you're having a hard time coming up with a list of people to ask to support your project, here are some ideas to get you going. You may be surprised at how many people you know and how many of them will be willing to give money to a good cause.

- **Family:** Parents, grandparents, kids, siblings, aunts, uncles, cousins, and in-laws.

- **Friends:** Your friends, friends of your friends, and friends of your spouse or partner.

- **Social acquaintances:** Old friends you see only on occasion. Friends from college or school. Your former professors or teachers. Friends from your old job. People from the hotline or community group where you used to volunteer.

- **Neighbors:** Next door, upstairs, downstairs, down the hall, the whole building! People on the block whom you always run into when you go jogging or walk the dog, or people you see at the grocery store. Your co-op board. Your tenants association. Your landlord. Your tenants. Your superintendent. Your babysitter. Your child care collective. Your car pool. The parents of your children's friends.

- **People from your house of worship:** Your religious leader. Members of the congregation. The people you share holidays with.

- **Colleagues:** People in your office. Your partners, your clients, your supervisor. Former partners, clients, supervisor. People who used to work in the office but recently left. Colleagues from community work. Union leaders, activists, your steward, your business agent, other union staff.

- **Club members:** From your block association, political club, book club, food co-op, local peace or environmental group. The PTA. Your local school board, civic organization, community board.

- **Leisure contacts:** Members of your bowling league, volleyball team, cooking group, pickup basketball crowd. The bridge club. Your poker buddies. Fellow students in night-class, in yoga class, at the gym. People from beach trips, camping trips. People you sing with in a choir or jam with or go caroling with. Your dance partner. People you walk with, garden with, vacation with.

- **Professionals and service providers:** Your barber or hairstylist, lawyer, dentist, doctor, chiropractor, pharmacist, broker, butcher, dry cleaner, baker. Your repairman or handyman. Your housecleaner, lawn service, pool service, heating and cooling maintenance crew. Your mechanic.

- **People on past lists:** The invitation list to your last party. Your holiday card list. The program from your last reunion. Your address books, at work and at home.

Handout C.1
Tips on Asking Individuals for Money

When you remember that people like to give money to causes they care about, you might be a little less nervous to ask them for support. If you're asking someone you know who is also someone who believes in the work you're doing, they're very likely to say yes, or at least be nice about saying no. Here are some tips on getting comfortable with asking for money.

- Prepare a list of people you would like to ask, using the forms provided in the relevant chapters, and start with the people you feel most confident about or who you're most comfortable approaching. Go to the ones who make you more nervous later, after you've had a little practice (and some success).

- Practice first with a friend.

- Ask for a specific amount of money or at least the range of gifts you're looking for.

- Be prepared to talk about why this cause is important to you. People like to hear about your personal relationship to the cause; they become inspired by your enthusiasm.

- Be open to any questions your potential supporters may have, and take an interest in what they care about.

- Don't worry about being able to answer every question a prospect may have. You can always tell them that you'll find out and get back to them with the answer.

- After you ask, stop talking! Wait for the person to respond. They may respond with a question or say they have to think about it, but don't assume you know what they're going to say.

- If they say yes, make a plan for how you're going to collect their payment.

- Always thank your prospects whether they give or not (for taking the time to think about it, for giving, for supporting you in whatever way they can).

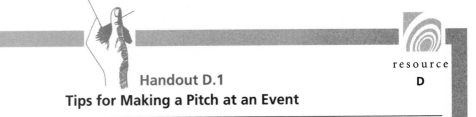

Handout D.1
Tips for Making a Pitch at an Event

At a community dinner or other public event or as part of a house party, the pitch for donations is often the most important part of the event. The following tips will help prepare you for that crucial moment.

- *Choose your moment.* Time the pitch so that the most people will be there when it is made and so it occurs at the point of highest energy in the program.

- *Keep it short and simple.* Your pitch will be more powerful if it is strong, from the heart, and to the point.

- *Dramatize.* Remind people what's at stake.

- *Be creative* about the ask. See below for ideas.

- Lead by example. *Have "plants"* who will pull out their checkbooks and declare the gift that they will make (if part of program) or place their contributions in the collection basket as people come around.

- *Make it easy.* Hand out an envelope, donation card or slip, and a pen to every person.

- *Collect the money.* Have a team of people politely but actively collect checks shortly after the pitch. Those collecting should hold baskets as they approach people, not just leave the basket on a table or even just pass it around. They should make sure that everyone is approached, looked in the eye, and thanked. Have someone with a basket stand at the door to catch every person as they leave.

IDEAS FOR DOING THE PITCH

Visioning exercise. "Close your eyes and picture . . ." Paint a vision of hope for the possibility of change in our community. Use humor—ask your audience to envision the project's work, then envision raising their hand, reaching into their pocket or purse to get their checkbook. Ask them to envision writing their lucky number down, then adding lots of zeroes to it.

Double what you came here to give. "If you came here thinking you would give $20, consider giving $40. If you came here to give $50, consider $100."

Challenge people to meet the goal. State the fundraising goal for the party and ask people to help you meet it. "Tonight we're trying to raise $1,000. How much can you give toward that goal?" Report back on how much you have raised and ask if people will pitch in more if you need just a little more to reach the goal. Celebrate when you reach the goal.

Lead with a gift. The person doing the pitch can lead with their own gift: "I am going to start off the night with a gift of (so many dollars)."

Have people announce their gifts. Ask people to stand up or raise their hands if they can give $200, $100, $50, $25.

Ask people to stretch. Ask people to contribute what is significant for them: "This issue is important, and that is why you are all here with us. I would like to ask you to think about why you care about this cause, and then make the biggest contribution you can, one that is truly significant for you."

Worksheet E.1
Volunteer Tracking Sheet

Name, address, phone, e-mail	Role they played	How they want to stay involved	Thanked?

For More Information

Periodicals

Chronicle of Philanthropy. www.philanthropy.com or (202) 466-1200.

Grassroots Fundraising Journal. www.grassrootsfundraising.org or (888) 458-8588.

Mal Warwick's Newsletter: Successful Direct Mail, Telephone, and Online Fundraising. www.malwarwick.com or (800) 217-7377.

Books

Flanagan, J. *The Grassroots Fundraising Book.* Chicago: Contemporary Books, 1992.

Klein, K. *Ask and You Shall Receive*: *A Fundraising Training Program for Religious Organizations and Projects.* San Francisco: Jossey-Bass, 2000.

Klein, K. *Como Recaudar Fondos en Su Comunidad.* Oakland, Calif.: *Grassroots Fundraising Journal*, 2002.

Klein, K. *Fundraising for Social Change.* (4th ed.) San Francisco: Jossey-Bass, 2000.

Klein, K. *Fundraising in Times of Crisis.* San Francisco: Jossey-Bass, 2003.

Klein, K., and Roth, S. *Raise More Money: The Best of the* Grassroots Fundraising Journal. San Francisco: Jossey-Bass, 2001.

Klein, K., and Roth, S. *The Board of Directors.* Oakland, Calif.: Grassroots Fundraising Journal, 2000.

Quatmann, V. *You Can Do It! A Volunteer's Guide to Raising Money for Your Group in Words and Pictures.* (Available in Spanish and English.) Maryville, Tenn.: Southern Empowerment Project, 2003. www.southernempowerment.org. or (865) 984-6500.

Robinson, A. *Selling Social Change (Without Selling Out): Earned Income Strategies for Nonprofits.* San Francisco: Jossey-Bass, 2001.

Warwick, M. *How to Write Successful Fundraising Letters.* San Francisco: Jossey-Bass, 2001.

Video

Ready, Set, Raise! Your Guide to Grassroots Fundraising, with Kim Klein and Russell Roybal. (Available in VHS and DVD formats.) Denver: Grassroots Institute for Fundraising Training, n.d. www.grassrootsinstitute.org.

Web Sites

CompassPoint Nonprofit Services. www.compasspoint.org.
> *A nonprofit training, consulting, and research organization in San Francisco and Silicon Valley offering a broad range of services that provide nonprofits with the management tools, concepts, and strategies necessary to shape change in their communities.*

Energize, Inc. www.energizeinc.com.
> *A training, consulting, and publishing firm specializing in volunteerism.*

Grassroots Fundraising Journal. www.grassrootsfundraising.org.
> *A bimonthly magazine that gives small organizations hands-on, how-to information on the wide range of fundraising strategies used to build a broad base of individual donors.*

Grassroots Institute for Fundraising Training. www.grassrootsinstitute.org.
> *Provides training, consultation, and an internship program to develop and strengthen the grassroots fundraising skills of individuals and organizations working for social justice, with an emphasis in communities of color.*

Groundspring. www.groundspring.org.
> *Internet-based information technology solutions to help nonprofit organizations raise funds and communicate with their stakeholders online and manage their operations more effectively.*

Technical Assistance for Community Services (TACS). www.tacs.org.
> *Provides training, consultation, information, and resources that nonprofits need to work better.*

TechSoup. www.techsoup.org.
> *A one-stop resource for nonprofit technology needs through free information, resources, and support; through their TechSoup Stock program, nonprofits can access donated and discounted technology products generously provided by corporate and nonprofit technology partners.*

Blank Worksheets, Workplans, and Scripts

Worksheets

Worksheet 4.1
Sample Form for Tracking Donors

Name	Address	Phone	E-mail	Amount donated	Date of donation	Fundraising strategy	Comments	Date thanked

Potential Supporters

Use this form to create your list of people to ask for a donation. Refer to Resource B, "Who Can You Ask?" to help you come up with ideas that may not have occurred to you. Once you've created your list, decide how much money you'll request from each person. If you have absolutely no idea, then suggest a range, such as $25–$100.

Name and contact info	Relationship to you	Cares about cause?	Gives away money?	How much to ask for

Worksheet 5.2
Tracking Form for Asks Made

Use this form to keep track of your requests for support. It's easy to forget who you called, when you left a message, and how much they said they'd give if you don't write it down.

Name of prospect	Date letter (or e-mail) sent	Date phone call(s) made	Result/notes	Amount pledged	Date $ received and amount	Date Thank you sent

Worksheet 6.1
Phonebank: Individual Tally Sheet

Volunteer Name: _____   Date: _____

Number of hours of calling (in 15-minute increments): _____

Results

Attempts:

Contacts:

Pledges or donations made:

Total amount: $_____

No:

"Take me off your list":

For each call you make, enter a tally mark for *all* of the relevant categories.

For example: 𝍪

Worksheet 6.2
Phonebank: Consolidated Tracking Sheet

Number of Volunteers: _____   Date: _____

Volunteer name	Volunteer hours	Attempts	Contacts	Donations	Total $ (credit cards)	Total $ (pledges)	Total $	Number of No's
Total								

Worksheet 6.3
Sample Call List

This is a list of names you have collected from your own database, from contacts of your volunteers, or from lists of organizations that are willing to share their names with you. This is the list from which your phonebankers will make their calls and record their results.

Name and address	Phone number	History and notes	Result of call	Pledge form sent (and date)	Money collected

What is the problem you are working to address?

What is the solution you propose?

What specific action steps are you asking people to take?

Who is most affected by your issue? Who else cares about this issue? How would you reach these groups? What neighborhoods do these groups live in?

Do you have volunteers with some experience asking for money or doing outreach to help coordinate and to canvass? Who are the other volunteers you would like to recruit?

What contribution levels will you ask for? What will be the payment method? What is your projected fundraising goal?

What follow-up do you have the capacity to do?

Worksheet 7.2
Individual Canvass Tracking Sheet

Use this sheet for each canvasser to track their results. If you are using clipboards or folders, you can tape this on the back so that they can easily make "hatchmarks" as they go. The End-of-Canvass Checklist reminds each person what they need to do before leaving.

Name: _____ Phone: _____

Where Canvassed: _____ Date: _____

Hour	Number of homes visited	Number of contacts	Number of actions	Number of gifts	Amount of cash	Amount of check
1						
2						
3						
Total						

End-of-Canvass Checklist

☐ Filled out individual tracking sheet

☐ Posted results on butcher paper

☐ Turned in all checks, credit cards, and cash

☐ Analyzed results in debrief

☐ Signed thank-you letters for people who gave today

Worksheet 7.3
Canvass Coordinator Report

Copy this sheet onto butcher or easel paper for canvassers to record their results after the canvass. They should transfer their results from the Individual Canvass Tracking Sheet onto the butcher paper. This way, during the debrief, everyone can see the collective results and analyze the day. The coordinator can use this sheet to track the results in case of future canvassing. The end-of-canvass checklist reminds the coordinator what to do before leaving.

Name: _____   Date: _____   Phone: _____   Where canvassed: _____

Name	Hours out	Number of homes visited	Number of contacts	Number of actions	Total number of gifts	Total amount of gifts	Checks	Cash
Total								

Evaluation of the Day
Strengths

Challenges

Solutions

End-of-Canvass Checklist
☐ Make sure people fill out their Individual Tracking Sheet.
☐ Collect pledges, checks or cash, and thank-you notes from canvassers.
☐ Double-check that everything is filled out and that the money matches the pledges.
☐ Double-check thank-you letters and send them out.
☐ Deposit checks.
☐ Make sure there is a follow-up plan for all action items.

Worksheet 8.1
House Party Tracking Sheet

Use this worksheet to keep track of invitations mailed, follow-up calls made, and whether people are coming. If people are not coming, ask them for a donation and write their pledge in the appropriate column.

Name	Address	Phone	E-mail	Invitation sent	Calls	Coming?	Pledge	Received	Notes

Use this worksheet with your dinner planning team to come up with fundraising goals, goals besides raising money, and resources. Then use the steps in the chapter and sample workplan to make a detailed plan.

What are our fundraising goals?

- Fundraising goal $_____$ – Costs $_____$ = Total (NET) $_____$
- How can we raise money from people/places that would not give otherwise?

  _____

  _____

- Can we get in-kind donations for the event?

  _____

  _____

- In addition to ticket sales, what are other ways to raise money at the dinner?

  ☐ Do pitch   ☐ Raffle   ☐ Ad book   ☐ Table sponsorship

  ☐ Silent auction   ☐ Other _____

  _____

What are our goals besides raising money? Do we want to:

- Increase our project's visibility? Celebrate victories? Thank and motivate people?
- Increase volunteer commitment, fundraising skills, other skills?

  _____

  _____

  _____

What resources do we have?

- How much money do we have up front? _____
- Who can we ask for money? _____

  _____

  _____

- How much time do we have to plan the event? _____
- Who can we recruit to help plan and run the event?

  _____

  _____

- Other resources:_____

Worksheet 9.2
Dinner Invitation, Turnout, and Donation Tracking

Use this worksheet to keep track of invitations mailed, follow-up calls made, and whether people are coming. If people are not coming, ask them for a donation and write their pledge in the appropriate column.

Name	Address	Phone	E-mail	Invitation sent	Calls	Coming?	Pledge	Received	Notes

Worksheet 10.1
Pledge Form for _____athon

Use this form to keep track of the people you solicit for sponsorships. Write down their name and contact information, and note the date that you complete each step in the process.

Sponsor's name and contact info (include phone and e-mail)	Date solicited (by letter, phone, or e-mail)	Date of follow-up and result	Amount pledged	Pledge collected (date and amount)

Worksheet 11.1
Auction Items Tracking Form

Name and contact info	Type of item	Date letter sent	Date of follow-up (call or in-person)	Result	Next steps, comments

Worksheet 12.1
Ad Sales Tracking Form

Each time a call is made or updated information is obtained from a prospect, note it on this form. With all the details involved in putting together an ad book, it is important to keep track of your progress.

Name and contact info	Date letter sent	Date of follow-up call and result	Size and fee	Ad copy received date	Payment received date	Notes

Worksheet 14.1
Raffle Prize Tracking Form

Name and contact info	Type of prize	Who will solicit and how?	Date solicitation made (and how)	Result	Next steps and comments

Worksheet 14.2
Raffle Ticket Tracking Form

Name _____ Number of tickets taken _____ Date _____

Check-in calls or e-mails	Date	Number of tickets sold	Funds collected ($)	Unsold tickets returned	Funds turned in ($)
	____	____	____		
	____	____	____		
Total:	____	____	____	Total: ____	____

Name _____ Number of tickets taken _____ Date _____

Check-in calls or e-mails	Date	Number of tickets sold	Funds collected ($)	Unsold tickets returned	Funds turned in ($)
	____	____	____		
	____	____	____		
Total:	____	____	____	Total: ____	____

Name _____ Number of tickets taken _____ Date _____

Check-in calls or e-mails	Date	Number of tickets sold	Funds collected ($)	Unsold tickets returned	Funds turned in ($)
	____	____	____		
	____	____	____		
Total:	____	____	____	Total: ____	____

Name _____ Number of tickets taken _____ Date _____

Check-in calls or e-mails	Date	Number of tickets sold	Funds collected ($)	Unsold tickets returned	Funds turned in ($)
	____	____	____		
	____	____	____		
Total:	____	____	____	Total: ____	____

Workplans

Workplan 5.1
The Personal Ask

What	Who	When (Week Number)									Done
		1	2	3	4	5	6	7	8	9	
1. Make a plan											
Create a gift-range chart											
2. Recruit volunteers											
3. Compile names of people to ask for $											
4. Prepare materials											
Sample letter, response form, envelopes											
5. Conduct training and orientation											
6. Send letters											
7. Make follow-up calls											
Meet with donors (for requests of $500+)											
Check in with volunteers											
8. Send thank you notes											
9. Evaluate											

Workplan 6.1
Phonebanks

What	Who	When (Week Number)								Done
		1	2	3	4	5	6	7	8	
1. Make a plan										
Make a budget										
Identify potential volunteer roles										
2. Recruit volunteers										
3. Compile lists of people to call										
4. Find a location										
Finalize site and date										
5. Prepare materials										
6. Make final preparations										
Make sure you have enough phone lines										

What	Who	When (Week Number)								Done
		1	2	3	4	5	6	7	8	
Arrange for refreshments										
Make reminder calls to volunteers										
7. Hold the phonebank										
Follow up on pledges made										
8. Wrap up										

Workplan 7.1
Door-to-Door Fundraising

What	Who	When (Week Number)								Done
		1	2	3	4	5	6	7	8	
1. Make a plan										
Identify coordinators										
Set fundraising and volunteer turnout goals										
Decide who and where to contact and how to talk about issue										
Picture the flow of the day										
Identify potential volunteer roles										
2. Recruit volunteers										
Make calls to recruit volunteers										
3. Secure logistics										
Identify space to do send-off and debrief										
Make transportation plan if needed										
4. Prepare materials										
Adjust the script to fit your issue										
Copy tracking sheets, informational flyers, and other needed papers										
Prepare all other materials needed for the day										

What	Who	When (Week Number)								Done
		1	2	3	4	5	6	7	8	
5. Prepare training for volunteers										
Recruit trainers										
Adjust training to fit your issue										
Do a test run of the canvass with coordinators and trainers										
6. Go out in the field										
Do training with volunteers on the day (or before, if needed)										
Go out in the field										
7. Evaluate, do paperwork, and follow up										
Debrief, evaluate, and celebrate with the volunteer team										
If possible, schedule one to three more canvassing sessions										
Do paperwork, document the event										
Send out thank-yous										

Workplan 8.1
House Party

What	Who	When (Week Number)						Done
		1	2	3	4	5	6	
1. Find a host and make a plan								
Recruit hosts								
Choose date, time, and location of house party								
Make a workplan and budget								
2. Prepare an invitation list								
Brainstorm as large an invitation list as possible								
Track down e-mails and addresses for invitees								
3. Prepare and send the invitation materials								
Prepare invitation and reply slip								
Mail invitations								
4. Make follow-up calls								
Make calls to confirm attendees, ask others to still give								
Two days before house party, make reminder calls								
5. Prepare the agenda, practice the pitch, and hold the party								
Prepare program and pitch								
Gather the materials needed for the party								
Buy and prepare food and refreshments								
Hold the party								
6. Send thank-yous								
7. Evaluate								

Workplan 9.1
Community Dinner

What	Who	When (Week Number)												Done
		1	2	3	4	5	6	7	8	9	10	11	12	
1. Make a plan and budget														
Plan overall vision and goals for dinner														
Make a budget														
Make a workplan														
Decide whether to do additional fundraising activities														
Identify potential volunteer roles														
2. Recruit volunteers														
Match volunteers with roles and responsibilities														
Provide training if needed														
Check in and provide ongoing support														
3. Develop invitation list														
Brainstorm invitation list with volunteers and others														
4. Find a dinner site and set date														
Decide on site needs: child care room, kitchen, size, and so on														
Call and visit potential sites														
Finalize site and date														
5. Design, print, and send invitations														
Design invitations (logistics, reply card, reply envelope)														
Print invitations and reply card, buy envelopes														
Have a mailing party														
6. Plan program														
Design program agenda														
Recruit and prep speakers and performers														
Arrange sound system														
Orchestrate the pitch														

Workplan 9.1
Community Dinner (continued)

What	Who	When (Week Number)												Done
		1	2	3	4	5	6	7	8	9	10	11	12	
7. Arrange food, drinks, and other logistics														
Get food and drink donations, decide whether to cook or cater														
Buy utensils and other necessary items														
Decide whether child care is needed and prepare														
Make a plan for getting into and closing up the dinner site														
Make any other needed arrangements														
8. Publicize event, do turnout calls, get contributions														
Volunteers sell tickets and get contributions from invitees														
Publicize dinner through newspaper, PSAs, flyers														
Compile and revise registration list														
9. Review event details and hold the event														
Do minute-by-minute breakdown and run through with key people														
Set up and clean up														
Hold the dinner														
10. Evaluation and thank-yous														
Evaluate and celebrate with volunteer team														
Document event														
Send out thank-yous														

Workplan 10.1
Bowlathon

What	Who	When (Week Number)										Done
		1	2	3	4	5	6	7	8	9	10	
1. Make a plan												
2. Recruit volunteers												
3. Set date and secure bowling lanes												
4. Conduct brief training or orientation for volunteers												
5. Check in with bowlers on pledge gathering												
6. Hold the bowlathon												
7. Follow up to collect pledges												
8. Evaluate and send thank-yous												

Workplan 11.1
Auction

What	Who	When (Week Number)											Done
		1	2	3	4	5	6	7	8	9	10	11	
1. Make a plan													
Make a budget													
Decide on live or silent auction (or both)													
Identify potential volunteer roles													
2. Recruit volunteers													
3. Prepare volunteers to solicit items													
4. Solicit auction items													
Make follow-up calls to volunteer solicitors													
5. Plan program and logistics													
Find a location													
Find an auctioneer (live auction only)													
Line up entertainment or speakers													
Make food and drink arrangements													
6. Publicize													
Design, print, and mail invitations													
Prepare other publicity (flyers, ads, e-mail)													
7. Make follow-up calls to invitees													
8. Make final preparations													
Prepare auction catalogue													
Set up for event													
Finalize the details: food, drink, people to help out													
9. Hold the auction													
10. Send thank-yous and evaluate													

Workplan 12.1
Ad Book

What	Who	When (Week Number)																Done
		1	2	3	4	5	6	7	8	9	10	11	12	13	14	15	16	
1. Make a plan																		
Decide what event or product ad book is for																		
Make a budget—printer estimate, set ad prices																		
Make a workplan																		
Identify potential volunteer roles																		
2. Recruit and train and volunteers																		
Recruit volunteers and match with roles and responsibilities																		
Provide training and set goals																		
Weekly check-in calls, support, sales updates																		
3. Brainstorm prospective advertisers																		
Have volunteers brainstorm people to sell ads to																		
Coordinate and match asks, size ad to ask for																		
4. Develop and mail sales packet																		
Develop letter, ad rates sheet, ad purchase form, and so on																		
Buy envelopes (letter and reply)																		
Have mailing party																		

Workplan 12.1 (continued)

What	Who	When (Week Number)																Done
		1	2	3	4	5	6	7	8	9	10	11	12	13	14	15	16	
5. Make follow-up calls																		
Make calls and get ad commitments																		
Send out sales packets as needed																		
Communicate results to coordinator, coordinator to give updates																		
Coordinator sends out invoices and thank-yous to advertisers																		
6. Get ad designs in																		
Make follow-up calls to get ad designs and payments																		
Deadline for ad designs																		
7. Produce ad book																		
Design ad book																		
Deadline to send ad book layout to printer																		
Printing																		
8. Distribute ad book																		
9. Evaluate and send thank-yous																		
Send all advertisers ad book and thank-you																		
Evaluate ad book with volunteer team																		
Document ad book plan, materials, sales, ads, contacts																		
Send out thank-yous to volunteers																		

Workplan 13.1
Car Wash

What	Who	When (Week Number)						Done
		1	2	3	4	5	6	
1. Make a plan								
Identify potential volunteer roles								
2. Recruit volunteers								
3. Find a location								
4. Set a date								
5. Plan additional fundraising activities (such as bake sale)								
6. Publicize								
7. Final preparations								
Reminder calls to volunteers								
8. Hold car wash								
9. Thank the volunteers								

Workplan 14.1
Raffle

What	Who	When (Week Number)											Done
		1	2	3	4	5	6	7	8	9	10	11	
1. Make a plan													
Make a budget													
Decide if stand-alone or part of event													
2. Recruit volunteers													
Prepare materials													
Orient volunteers													
Come up with ideas for raffle prizes													
Draft forms and sample letters													
3. Solicit raffle prizes													
Make follow-up calls to volunteer solicitors													
4. Design and print tickets													
5. Distribute tickets to volunteers													
6. Follow up with ticket sellers													
7. Collect money and ticket stubs													
8. Hold the drawing													
9. Send out prizes and thank-yous and evaluate													

Workplan 15.1
Garage Sale

What	Who	When (Week Number)							Done
		1	2	3	4	5	6	7	
1. Make a plan									
Set fundraising goal and create budget									
Identify potential volunteer roles									
2. Recruit volunteers									
3. Find a location									
Finalize location and date									
4. Solicit donated items to sell									
Find place to store items (before sale)									
Arrange for item dropoffs or pickups									
5. Publicize sale									
6. Make final preparations									
7. Hold the sale									
8. Wrap up									
9. Send thank-yous									

Scripts

Script 5.1
Sample Phone Script for Follow-Up Calls

Structure of what to say	What to say
Introduction—who you are, brief greeting, purpose of call	
Explain problem and what you're raising money for; speak briefly about the project you're raising money for	
Ask if they have questions	
Ask for a contribution	
If they say yes	
If they say no	
If they hesitate or seem unsure	
Thank them!	

Script 6.1
Sample Phone Script

Structure of what to say	What to say
Introduction	
If they say no	
If they say they're not interested	
If they say yes, explain why you're calling and engage them	
If they don't know about it, continue	
Check in to see if they have any questions	
Make the ask!	
Stop and listen. Pause until they say something. If they say yes, they'd like to give	
If they say no	

Script 7.1
Sample Conversation at the Door

The basic structure of a conversation at the door that is outlined here can be applied to any issue you want to canvass on. Your volunteers should use this as a guideline, but emphasize to them that they should be conversational and not read from this outline.

Structure of what to say	What to say
Introduction—who you are, the organization you represent, what you are there for, what you want	
Problem—one- or two-sentence summary of the problem that you are organizing around. In this section, confirm the person's support	
Solution—one or two sentences to educate the person as to what your organization is doing about it	
Confirmation	
Bridge—link the person's agreement with the issue to the need to make a contribution	

Structure of what to say	What to say
The ask—ask for a specific amount, and be straightforward	
If they say no, provide options, connect the money and the issue, and close the deal. Identify why they are saying no. Respond by acknowledging their issue, reassuring them, connecting the issue and money, and by providing options.	
If they say yes	
Action piece—it is important to get people to take action besides giving money. Do this *after* asking for money.	
Thank them!	

Script 8.1
House Party Turnout Call Script

Structure of the call	What to say
Opening—you're calling people you know, so be yourself and chat. Be friendly, but make sure to move to the house party. Tell them why you're calling: to follow up on the invitation to your house party.	
Remind them of the details: Tell them when and where the house party is and ask directly if they can come.	
If they can't come, ask them to make a donation.	
If they are planning to come, remind them of the logistics and to bring their checkbooks.	
Thank them!	

Script 12.1
The Follow-Up Call

Structure of what to say	What to say
Introduction	
If no	
If yes, explain why you're calling and engage the prospect	
If yes, move directly to the ask	
If the prospect is not familiar with your group	
Make the ask	
Stop and listen. Pause until they say something. If the answer is yes, they'll buy an ad	
If they say no	
If they say, "Maybe," or "I have to think about it," or "I have to talk to my business partner"	

THE AUTHORS

STEPHANIE ROTH is the editor of the bimonthly *Grassroots Fundraising Journal* and coeditor, with Kim Klein, of the compilation *Raise More Money: The Best of the Grassroots Fundraising Journal.* Roth is also a trainer and consultant in fundraising and board development. She has worked as a staff member, board member, volunteer, and consultant with nonprofit organizations in the United States and overseas since 1978, with an emphasis on grassroots organizations working for social justice.

Roth was one of the founding staff members of the Grassroots Institute for Fundraising Training (GIFT); other staff positions have included director of the Long Island Technical Assistance Center and codirector of New York Women Against Rape. She lives in Berkeley, California, and serves on the board of Jewish Voice for Peace.

MIMI HO is the program director of the Asian Pacific Environmental Network (APEN), which organizes low-income Asians and Pacific Islanders in California around issues of environmental justice in the workplace and home. She has been a trainer and consultant in fundraising, organizing campaigns, and organizational development. Previously, Ho worked as an organizer and codirector of Californians for Justice during electoral fights against several racist, antiyouth, and antiworker ballot initiatives in the 1990s.

Ho comes to grassroots fundraising from a community organizing perspective, which stresses the need to fund dynamic, political, community organizing projects; the method of bringing lots of everyday community members together to take action; and the belief that everyone can do it!

RESOURCES FOR SOCIAL CHANGE
AVAILABLE FROM JOSSEY-BASS AND CHARDON PRESS

Raise More Money:
The Best of the Grassroots Fundraising Journal

Kim Klein, Stephanie Roth, Editors

Whether you are a new or seasoned fundraiser, this collection of the best articles from the *Grassroots Fundraising Journal* will provide you with new inspiration to help bring in more money for your organization. Filled with strategies and guidance, this unprecedented anthology shows you how small nonprofits can raise money from their communities and develop long-term financial stability.

Paperback   ISBN: 0-7879-6175-2

Fundraising for Social Change

4TH EDITION

Kim Klein

This classic how-to fundraising text teaches you what you need to know to raise money from individuals. Learn how to set fundraising goals based on realistic budgets; write successful direct mail appeals; produce special events; and raise money from major gifts, planned giving, capital campaigns, and more.

Paperback   ISBN: 0-7879-6174-4

The Nonprofit Membership Toolkit

4TH EDITION

Ellis M. M. Robinson

Step by step, *The Nonprofit Membership Toolkit* shows how to create, manage, and sustain a dynamic membership program that will help a social change organization thrive. Written for both new and well-established social change organizations, this book is grounded in proven marketing techniques. It gives managers and executive directors the information and tools needed to understand their current members and attract new ones, and it walks organizations through the process of linking program goals with membership goals.

Paperback   ISBN: 0-7879-6506-5

Notes